INTRODUCTION

Over the years the Anarchist Teapot mobile kitchen was often asked for advice on mass catering. I got tired of writing the same stuff over and over again in emails, so I took it on to compile an info booklet. I thought about 10 people would be interested in it, but we've printed and reprinted countless copies – for some bizarre reason, there seems to be a lot of you interested in cooking massive pots of vegan food.

So here's a new and updated reprint. Some things had gone a bit out of date, and I've also tried to re-organise the zine so it'd be more useful for cooking in different settings, not just a field. Some disclaimers to start with - this is entirely based on our own, specific experiences, and what I'd reply if you asked me how to cook for 150 people? It's also entirely based on our own motivation to cook. To us, it's not to do with making profits or usually even paying ourselves, but entirely to do with wanting to fulfil a role in the communities we build when we engage in grassroots resistance to the status quo. And we've found feeding people delicious food is a great way of consolidating community.

We set up – 20 years ago now! - because we thought that a movement serious about attacking authority, confronting exploitation and destruction, and building a new world, should be able to take care of itself including feeding ourselves at events and mobilisations. The Teapot was based within the anarchist and ecological movements, and we didn't consider ourselves separate, some kind of service or vending machine.

We've since seen a bit of a decline in mass mobilisations of the kind our kitchen came in useful for, and the collective grew older but not bigger, so we've passed on our really big pans to Veggies and just occasionally cook at events now. We've not lost our passion for cooking though and

1

you'll still find us in a social centre kitchen, field or a conference, just less often! Compared to commercial catering work, Teapot-style cooking on a voluntary basis, i.e. when it's not a 'job' with a manager and all that shit, but self organised and on our own terms, is hugely enjoyable and satisfying, even when it's hard work.

We've also always taken pride in providing decent, nutritious food that's vegan, organic, or at least good quality, locally sourced and affordable. It's not just monied Guardian supplement readers that deserve to eat well, after all!

The Anarchist Teapot - history and set up

The Teapot started off as a series of squatted cafés in Brighton, England, back in 1996, offering a 'collective front room' with tea, sometimes food by donation, radical reading materials and events. We kind of ran out of good buildings to squat, and started looking for a permanent, legal space which led to the founding of the Cowley Club co-operative social centre in Brighton, but that's whole a different story.

As a squat café we sometimes got asked to cook at events. So we obliged, and ended up getting support and advice from our friends from Holland, the anarchist catering collective Rampenplan. After helping them cook at an Earth First! summer gathering in 1998, we were ready to set up as a mobile activist kitchen.

Our first meals were shit. Hopefully no one remembers them (though SOME people still make jokes about how long kidney beans should be cooked....). Gradually we learnt how to avoid disasters, and over the years we continued cooking at the EF! Gatherings, plus everywhere and anywhere from free festivals - which we soon gave up doing - to community events in Brighton, gatherings for the co-operative network Radical Routes... we've cooked at demonstrations, squatted genetics test sites, climate camps and other action camps, international mobilisations. We even almost ended up hired to do the catering at the Green Party conference in Brighton.... but that's another long story... Our biggest set ups were in collaboration with other kitchens, coordinating the effort to feed thousands protesting against the G8 summits in Scotland in 2005 and Germany in 2007.

We've cooked in all sorts of places: squats and community centres, at camps, running after people with a pasting table and boxes of pasties at demonstrations. Cooking for an event over a few days, we'd do breakfast, lunch and dinner with tea and coffee on tap most of the time. We used to charge a max of £5/day for this but food cost has noticeably increased over time, and today we charge more like £7. At some events we'd just ask for donations, and this generally worked out quite well. Sometimes we wouldn't break even on an event (mostly due to orga-nisers overestimating numbers of people attending and us buying in too much food). We cook vegan, and try to buy mostly organic ingredients, depending on our budget and how much people are willing to pay.

We'd always have a few core members, some of which were involved since squat café times, and then others who like to cook and come along to events occasionally. It was always hard to find people willing to take on full responsibility for cooking – chopping help no problem, someone to help plan the menu or sort out getting ingredients, not so easy.

We did always rely on casual chopping and washing up helper armies, running around on a site trying to entice people into the kitchen to give us a hand for a couple hours. This is mainly where our interaction with what was going on occurred – we'd get to hear from our temporary volunteers what had happened, what plans were being drawn up, where they were from and their own stories. You always found the best people in the kitchen tent!

We sometimes brought a bookstall along, sometimes we offered workshops too. And we always liked to listen to loud music while we cooked.

VEGGIES
Catering Campaign (Nottingham)

Veggies was started in 1984 by members of the local animal rights group involved in campaigning at McDonalds and wishing to make vegan food readily accessible. They started with a mobile van parked outside the Pork Farms factory, then applied for a street trading permit to set up a catering trailer 6 days a week on a city centre market. A freezer service has also been consistently providing frozen supplies to other caterers, mainly via regional wholefood wholesalers, Lembas. An informal wholefood collective is also run for volunteers.

In June 2001 with the opening of a new base at the Sumac Centre, an autonomous community resource centre, café and social club, Veggies gave up its daily street stall to concentrate on event catering, from table-top scale catering at protests and buffets for local community groups meetings, to catering stalls at major events including Green Gatherings and Glastonbury Green Futures Field. This change of emphasis also enabled Veggies to provide more full weekend catering to campaign gatherings, whether hosted at the Sumac Centre or elsewhere, including Radical Routes, Rising Tides, Genetic Engineering Network etc. A popular café space has also be provided at Earth First and Animal Rights gatherings, alongside Anarchist Teapot's field kitchen.

Equipment-wise, we have two catering trailers that are used to provide pay-as-you-go catering at festivals, fairs and some national demos. A mini-marquee and a tabletop market stall are available to provide additional space at major events. Gas burners and cook pots are available to provide field kitchens and catering for gatherings for up to 150 people. Buffets for 10 -50 people are prepared in the self contained basement kitchen at the Sumac Centre, stretching to deluxe party buffets for up to 100.

For protest events on-the-streets we tend to provide pre-prepared pasties, cakes and drinks from a table top, bike trailer or simply tray-boxes 'on the run'. Payment is often by donation on a d-i-y self-serve basis. For more established events or pre-arranged demo locations we add home-made veggie burgers, hot drinks and other fair-trade snacks, individually priced from 50p - £2.50. For gatherings meals include curries, vegetable soups, ratatouille, vegetable stews etc with rice, cous-cous, pasta etc and fresh salads, breads and spreads. Subject to travel costs, numbers etc the cost for a full week-end may be around £10.

Festivals, fairs and commercial buffets raise the funds to subsidise campaign catering. We also pay towards the Sumac Centre's mortgage, finance the library/bookstall and provide other campaign resources, including internet services for local and national campaigns. Although losses may occur, for example if a protest does not go to plan, other events tends to raise sufficient to cover running costs. However funds are usually at a minimum before the 'summer season' begins. We aim to maintain an emergency reserve, invested with Radical Routes and the Sumac Centre. We have two workers job-sharing a minimum wage, minimum hours position to look after day-to-day organisation, doing associated campaign activities in their 'spare time'. Members with cookery skills prepare recipes and arrange menus. Others do education and media work, and give other technical backup. Local volunteers assist with many local campaign events and a nationwide network of volunteers is on call for events further afield. With local buffets, club nights and in-house events at the Sumac Centre, Veggies is usually busy throughout the year; during the summer up to three major events may occur each weekend.

Publicity for events supported by Veggies is provided on the detailed diary and linked archive at www.veggies.org.uk/diary.htm. Although originally 'caterers to animal rights movement', Veggies now works with a wide range of groups and campaigns for social justice, environmental protection, human rights and peace issues.

Veggies, 245 Gladstone Street, Nottingham NG7 6HX, UK
Phone : 0845 458 9595 - www.veggies.org.uk

SO HOW DO WE COOK FOR LOTSA PEOPLE THEN??

These are things to consider, but we're not offering a blueprint, just some ideas! Obviously slightly different points will apply depending on whether you're setting up an action kitchen, just looking to cook for an event or two, or establishing a community cafe.

SETTING UP A COLLECTIVE

Cooking can be hard work, but it's a lot less stressful, and more enjoyable, if you have a cooking posse consisting of people who get on well and feel some sort of affinity with each other. Not everyone needs to be the best cook, a whole range of skills come in useful for mass catering.

You don't need tons of you either; you can take on quite a lot with just a small core group of people, because you will probably be able to get random people to help with the labour intensive work such as chopping veg and cleaning up at an event you're cooking at. It's nice to be able to involve people attending an event in the kitchen - it makes it feel less like 'service' and more like a part of what's going on. If you are volunteer based, make this clear when you're cooking - if there's a programme, get it mentioned in it, and/or have a board explaining what you're about (everyone will assume you are a commercial enterprise otherwise, it beign capitalism and all).

There's been whole books written about consensus decision making and non hierarchical organising, so I won't go into it much here. Basically, it's nice to work together on a project such as a mobile kitchen, make decisions together, and divide up responsibilities in a fair and equal manner.

6

A c/o address could come in useful (also for setting up trade accounts with food suppliers, if needed), plus your usual communication tools.

Any business handling food is legally supposed to be registered with the local authority, which involves having an address and an inspection of your registered premises, a named 'manager' (though in most places, ID doesn't seem to be required), and filling out a form, then getting a visit from food hygiene officials and complying with their requirements. In the UK this only applies to a business that serves food on a regular basis, which is not clearly defined. Irregular food handling and on a small scale is exempt. So if you can claim that you are only an occasional caterer, you don't need to be registered. And, if you *can* stay under the radar, then do!

EQUIPMENT

Equipment will cost money, so you'll need some of that too. You may want to do some fundraising, or borrow money off someone and pay it back after you've generated some surplus from catering. Maybe you can apply for a grant, for example through a local authority small grants programme (stress the community aspect, etc). We did this years ago and got to buy lots of things and get food hygiene training as well. You can start off with the bare minimum of equipment and improve your set up as you go along.

Put word out that you're looking for catering equipment - people may find things in squats, or tat things for you. If you have any contacts with a recycling/second hand furniture/clearance business, let them know you're after catering stuff. Look in the free ads, in second hand catering shops/warehouses, restaurant supply shops, and on ebay/gumtree. You may even come across a fully kitted mobile catering van/trailer someone's fed up with if this suits what you want to do, or you might happen to squat somewhere with most or all of a kitchen in it!

Find a commercial catering supplies company that will send you a catalogue (you'll have to say you're a new food business). They all seem to be the same (Nisbets is the main one in the UK), and expensive for most things, but they'll at least give you an idea on what kind of equipment you could be wanting and looking around for.

If you're only going to cater once in a while, or usually for small events but one off for a big one, you might want to look round for a catering equipment hire place that's not too expensive. Bear in mind you'll really need to take care of the stuff and if these bloody anarcho types never bother bringing back your hired plates you will be coughing up a bomb on lost deposits.

INDOOR COOKING

So you might have a big dingy squat, a fancy cafe you can use, a community centre kitchen or whatever, so you don't need to build a kitchen from scratch but you can use what's there. A decent cooker makes a big difference – ideally gas rings and even better industrial standard, a double sink with hot water, some wipe-clean work surfaces and a moppable floor, and you're good to go. Figure out how and where you are going to safely store your food (pest proof, and in adequate temperatures), and all your equipment.

Other things to consider cooking indoors is that you may be subject to a food hygiene inspection, so make sure you've got good practises and put some thought into your kitchen set up. For example, it's good to separate veg prep including veg washing from the washing up; ideally you have a whole separate washing up area to prevent cross contamination (and chaos!), PLUS a seperate handwash sink. It's also good practise to keep surfaces clear and tidy, and regularly clean inside cupboards, underneath things, clear out out of date food and so on! Keep on top of it regularly and it won't all turn into a festering hellhole.

OUTDOOR COOKING

A general outdoor cooking setup for mass catering requires a tent or van or something to cook in, all your furniture (e.g. tables/work surfaces, seating, storage), a tap, ideally some electrical hookup, alongside your kitchen equipment which will include burners and large pans and the other things you'll need both indoors and outdoors.

Burners and Pans

The most important yet most difficult thing to get, especially on a budget. You may need to look around a lot until you find some decent stuff – check out catering supplies stores/second hand/auctions (e.g. specialist catering auctions)/and ebay. Stainless steel with a heavy bottom is best. You might find a large stockpot with a thin bottom - you'll only be able to use this for water/very liquidy stuff, because anything else will burn like fuck in it. As a guideline for volume, you can calculate 400ml/1.5 cups per portion, so a 25 litre pan will feed about 60 people – though the bigger the better.

Try to take care of your pans and frying pans - don't scrape them with sharp things, avoid excessive burning and then excessive scouring, and bending them out of shape, especially the bottom.

If you do get any really large pans, bear in mind you'll need burners that can handle the weight when full. You can get decent propane powered single ring gas burners that can take a fair bit of weight (ask in the shop) from some hardware stores, costing about £40-£50 – you can get even cheaper ones on ebay but they won't be as sturdy. Make sure they have tall enough legs to not sit too close to the ground. Gas burners need to be standing on a non-flammable surface that can withstand heat when in use! So, hard ground, grass (it may catch fire round it first, but then go out and stay out), paving slabs, or stone floor is best or if you are using it on a surface, make sure it can take the weight and is fire retardent.

Burners also need a bit of looking after, e.g. wiping the rust off with a wire brush. You can also get camping cookers with two or more rings - again, propane is more powerful than butane, and rings with lots of little holes (hm, maybe they have a special name) are better than the gas rings normal cookers have.

Make sure you have 'sets' i.e. three burners with 3 pans that fit on each of them well, rather than 20 small pans and 2 giant burners, or 2 small burners and 3 giant pans, etc. you get the picture. The more sets and volume you have, the more you can do!

When setting up at an event, you'll need **gas bottles**. Find out what your burner needs exactly, in terms of size of gas bottle and connection and make sure your gas bottle and regulator match. Orange propane bottles are usually more powerful than blue butane. Screw the pipe into the gas bottle tightly with a large adjustable spanner, threaded the 'wrong' way around (i.e. NOT lefty-loosy righty-tighty like everything else), and then test all connections for leaks: use a bit of washing up liquid in some water, turn gas on and pour the liquid over the connection - if it bubbles up, there's a leak. Turn off, and try fitting it again, then test again. Plumbers' tape(called PTFE in Britain) can help on a small leak you can't get rid of, but when you get home you should check it out. Multiple burners can all be connected to a single gas bottle, instead of using multiple gas bottles uneconomically, by using splitters to split the gas lines to feed into one bottle - ask at hardware stores, it's fairly easy.

If you're cooking outdoors, keep the gas bottles outside of your tent but make them as inaccessible as possible to random drunk people and children. Make sure you turn the gas bottles shut at night/when not in use for any length of time, and 'bleed' your burners after you have done this, i.e. let the gas left in the line out so it doesn't build up when you re-open the gas flow the next day and then explode in your face.

Rocket stoves and the like

This bit is nicked from a kitchens skillshare document created for the Climate Camp 2008. I don't know shit about these things so I have reproduced this as I tend to agree... *Wood chip fuelled rocket stoves are becoming a common sight around field kitchens and they can be very useful for heating water. Advice on their construction can be found on the internet and skill shares are common around the environmental movement and social centres. At current capacity it can be suggested that they are generally best kept as a supplement or reserve heat source, though as the technology and experience moves on this may change. Their advantages are sustainability and DIY/recycling ethos. However it is good to bear in mind that they are not often big, powerful or stable enough to support large pots and pans, they need constant tending and fuel monitoring and they make everything turn black and messy. Propane burners remain more reliable and you do not need to get in vast amounts of wood fuel.*

Field ovens

A good oven is not only useful to bake things in, but also to keep food warm, and it massively expands your cooking repertoire, beyond the realm of mere slop. For outdoor cooking, you might be able to get your hands on a small portable oven or mobile ones from army surplus - we have one that's like an insulated stainless steel box you can put on top of a burner. It's not that big but we can make garlic bread or keep sausages warm in it. Veggies use a decent 6-ring gas cooker on a gas bottle but it's fucken heavy and not very mobile. Or you may want to build your own one on site, for example a lovely earth pizza oven... Plenty of instructions for things like that online and worth doing if you have the time/a space for it.

Hosepipe

An indispensible item if you have really large pans, both to fill them up with water, to wash them up after, or to connect to a tap that's outside the kitchen. Hosepipes will need to be food grade, i.e. not just garden hose which taints the water and makes it taste icky. You can get them from camping/caravan shops. They will also need fittings, one at the end of the tap - don't skimp on the quality of the jubilee clip/fitting you use, if the water supply's powerful it'll burst off and you'll be constantly running out getting drenched fitting a crap one back on - and something on the other end that suits your needs, like a spray tap, a multi function one, whatever. After an event, drain your hosepipe (you don't want to store it full of water getting manky inside) and leave to dry if you can. Before an event, rinse it out before using. We have a hose that flattens when empty, so it can be wound up on a reel and not take up too much storage space.

A couple of water containers are useful too, one to put out with fresh tap water for drinking (it's annoying when people are constantly coming through your workspace to get some drinking water) and maybe another for your own handwash in the kitchen. You can get them from camping shops or second hand.

GENERAL KIT

Frying

Frying things for hundreds of people doesn't always work and is pretty tedious, but a frying pan is always useful, if just to toast seeds or fry up some garlic. You can get good sized wok style frying pans from some Asian shops. Flat ones are more useful (especially if you ever want to fry burgers) than the typical curved wok but you might like both. Remember to season it well (where you gently heat oil in it, then wipe it off or let it dry to build up a non stick layer) and avoid scouring it down.

A large griddle could be a good investment if you aspire to be a fry cook. The electric ones use a lot of power but for a field setup our Dutch friends have some excellent gas powered griddles.

Electrical appliances

Even when you're in the middle of a field, you might have access to some leccy - it's a good idea to have a good, long extension lead in your kit - for lighting, a stereo, and appliances. We try not to overdo it on appliances, both in terms of alt power availability (e.g. high energy users such as water boilers and fridges) and because it just gets silly.

A **food processor** is really handy though - don't expect to be sat there pureeing 100 litres of soup in it, but you could use it for mincing garlic, ginger and other additions, blending salad dressing, making vegan mayo or pesto, and also for shredding cabbage or grating (and you will be so happy not to hand grate. It completely sucks to grate 25 kilos of carrots by hand). Try to find one with a big bowl, and a decent wattage, though obviously very high wattage means you won't be able to use it on alt power.

An electric **hand blender** is good for whizzing up salad dressings and small amounts of soup. It's worth getting a blender with a brand name - we've thrown away more cheap, no-brand blenders than you can possibly imagine, but gotten a fair bit of life out of a Braun one we got on sale somewhere for a tenner. We don't usually use it straight in a hot pan but scoop out some out, blend it, then pour it back in, because the hot steam from the pan can fuck the blender.

Non electric alternatives to food processors and hand blenders include mandolin graters, and hand turned mincers. You may be able to get different attachments for these such as slicers and graters and mincers. If they're fairly large they can be quite efficient.

Things like rice cookers, deep fat fryers, juicers, electric whisks, toasters, grills, or soup kettles may be useful depending on your usual menus.

If you're cooking things but not serving them straight away or serving over a period of time, you'll need some way of keeping food at the right temperatures (i.e. hot or cold). You can either just not do such large amounts at a time and/or reheat things, or invest in some kind of fridge, and/or bain maries (pots sat in water that's kept hot), hotplates or chafing dishes. These aren't cheap new so if you want these, look for them second hand.

Microwaves use all the leccy, they don't really cook anything, and they make food taste icky too.

Cutlery, Crockery, Mugs

This also depends on how and what you want to cook and for how many - you might just do burgers in napkins and/or use disposable stuff. But disposable stuff = big waste over time, and it may become a good idea to invest in some crockery. You can also try getting people to bring their own mug, cutlery and crockery to an event, and just have some as backup for the inevitable few who will forget theirs. Make sure this gets put on the publicity for the event and people get plenty of reminders.

When buying crockery and mugs in bulk from a shop, always ask for a bulk discount. Store and transport your crockery etc. in sturdy plastic crates that let air through (for drying) and preferably stack well. After cooking at your first event you'll probably end up with a bunch of plastic crates that your veg/bread came in which are ideal for storage, or ask at places like a veg market for spare ones.

Plates/bowls: Proper porcelain plates might be easy to come by - second hand, tatted, from friends - but are a bastard to carry in large numbers if you are travelling to an event, and they do crack and break when chucked around in lots of washing up. Plates with chips and cracks will not pass a potential food hygiene inspection either. The Teapot first used tin/enamel camping style dishes, which are low, wide bowls - they have come in handy to serve both soup and main meals in, though they're a bit unsatisfying for proper meals. They have the advantage of stacking and taking up the minimum of space in storage, plus being fairly light to lug around. We use hard plastic plates now. Also not heavy, nicer for a big meal, pretty much stackable, cheap and replaceable, and don't break that easily.

There's two main types, hard transparent plastic that looks slightly

14

rubbery (hopefully you know what I mean, toddlers' drinking mugs are often made out of this stuff). They're good, but you do need to wash them up well and they get scratches from forks and knives. Then there's hard non-transparent plastic (that doesn't look rubbery) which is what we've been using, they scratch less and are more 'wipe clean', but they do have a tendency to just crack down the middle leaving a sharp edge of death. We got them all pretty cheap though, we found stacks of them in poundshops (sold as picnic plates).

Another option are steel bowls and plates of the Asian kind, ask around in Asian/Indian shops. They're usually light and you may get a good deal on them.

Cutlery: Easy to come by from second hand shops, and motorway service stations... Also, the simplest kinds aren't that expensive new and in packs of dozen from catering suppliers e.g. Nisbets (£2.50-£4 per dozen for forks or spoons, a bit more for knives). We keep ours in small blue, stackable crates that mushrooms and some other veg come in - they're ideal, cos again they let air through and muck out.

Mugs: Stainless steel stackable mugs are wonderful, but expensive. Sigh. One day we'll get them. We started off with enamel mugs (to suit our enamel bowls) because they were light and we got them cheap, but after a few years they went minging. Now we just look around for mug bargains in poundshops (4 for a pound etc). It does get heavy to lug around all these mugs, and they lose their handles and get chipped, but we haven't found a better solution so far. You might also like using the hard plastic 'picnic' mugs though I think they're weird to drink tea out of (but that's just me). Low bread or veg crates with a tightish mesh are the best thing to store mugs in - ask at a bakery or keep them after your first bread delivery... They stack, let air through to help mugs dry, and are just the right height for mugs.

We've lost more mugs than you can possibly imagine over the years. At every event, we leave with up to a whole crate less. Even when we go round the whole building/campsite collecting mugs, or offer children 5p for every mug they bring back... We have also used deposit systems, where mugs are kept behind our serving area and people have to come

15

and ask for a mug and leave a deposit. This can work okay, you also at least may have money left at the end to buy new mugs with for the ones that went walkies, but it does involve someone being approachable for mugs all day which can be a tedious job.

Utensils

You'll need stirrers that are long enough to handle your pans. If you have really, really big pans, you can get long paddle type ones from catering suppliers but they're expensive (we did manage to get two - 45 quid each!!! - from the grant we got...), but you can also make your own. To start with, we took a pair of wooden oars, sanded them down, and cut out holes in the paddle to make them look like big plastic tea stirrers. Just don't store them anywhere damp - you'll get mould on them.

Lots of long wooden spoons come in handy too.

We got a couple of big, 5 litre ladles from Rampenplan that they'd welded themselves. This is the one piece of our tat that people really seem to get impressed by. It's proved indispensable for scooping water and food in and out of pans, it also has a hook to hang it up, because you don't want to put it down on the ground, then pick it up again and dip in the soup. You can also just use a small pan for scooping though, with a handle with a hole or hook on it to hang it up after use.

Instead of lifting a big pan full of hot water and taking it somewhere to drain, it's often easier to just turn off the heat, leave the pan where it is, and scoop out the veg/pasta/rice with a scoopy thing. You can get big, curved, wire mesh scoops/spiders from Asian catering shops that do this job, the bigger the better. Using sturdy wire mesh baskets used for deep fat frying to scoop things out might work too.

A large colander is still a handy thing to have, for washing salad or draining from smaller pans. Other things include: serving spoons both

16

perforated and plain, tongs, ladles, fishslices (for frying, and serving up burgers or bakes), whisk, graters, scissors, salad spinner, peelers; all are essential or at least pretty damn useful. If you're baking, you'll also want a good spatula, sieve/sifting device, scales, measuring jug, and wire cake cooling trays.

Either get a good quality, larger garlic crusher, or just chop by hand or in a food processor. Crap garlic crushers are frustrating and break quickly. The same goes for tin openers. If you're doing a lot of tin opening, especially on large size tins, a normal, a cheap crap opener will give up very quickly. Invest in a decent tin opener or a surface mounted one.

Water Boilers

We'll talk about making coffee later (such a pain but obviously vital), but a few notes on urns here. If you have a good electricity supply, an electric urn/water boiler is a god piece of tat. New water boilers of the standard Burco variety cost about £100 and they are also pretty easy to pick up second hand (but they do break easily, so check they work before buying). They need watching and refilling (don't let them boil dry!). While the urn's not boiled yet, put a mug over the spout to stop people helping themselves to disappointing cups of non-tea. When it's boiled, turn it down as low as possible to stop it steaming like crazy and wasting leccy.

A good non electric alternative are gas powered water boilers, which cost about £200 new. If you're talking about catering for hundreds of people, you'll either need a number of electric urns, or you can also opt for using insulated ones filled with hot water or ready made teas and coffee (thereby avoiding using thousands of teabags). See the Hot Drinks section in the recipes for how we do this.

Chopping boards

You'll need quite a few of these, especially if you'll be trying to get people to come help you chop, and it's worth looking round for large sturdy ones. Wooden ones are fine, but food hygiene requirements involve colour coded hard plastic chopping boards – in the UK, it's green for salad vegetables, brown for root vegetables (cos they leave bits of dirt in the board, then that gets on salad veg that won't get cooked), and white for bread and dairy. If a chopping board is getting really scratched up, you should either chuck it, cos it won't pass any food hygiene inspection and that's for a reason, or clean it with a chopping board scraper which I've never seen in action so I have no idea what I'm talking about right now. But they exist. If you're using boards to put hot things on, use wooden, not plastic ones!

Knives

Again, something worth investing in - cheap, flimsy knives are false economy, and they just won't cut it (Ha. Ha.). We like Sabatier and Global which are expensive but we've had two Sabatier sets (5 knives for ca. £100) for over 15 years and they're still really good. A few cheap knives are good to have around for doing things like opening packets or peeling garlic with. Take good care of knives - keep them in a knife block or a canvas wallet or a knife box (also when transporting them - knives potentially flying round the back of a van doesn't sound very safe). It's very important to sharpen them regularly, once they lose their sharp edge, they'll stay blunt forever. Learn how to use a knife sharpener steel, or get yourself a pull through knife sharpener. You can only sharpen sharp-ish knives with a sharpener, so if they are pretty blunt they will need the edge re-grinding with a stone which is a good thing to learn how to do, and a stone is not expensive to buy. Do NOT let anyone use a good knife to cut boxes open, open tins, cut through wires, as a screwdriver, or anything like that. Threaten death.

Bowls and boxes, plastic stuff

Food storage boxes, the larger and the more the better, with lids, food grade (i.e not toxic on food), and stackable are indispensable for keeping chopped veg until use, washing veg in, serving salads, etc. We've been using large square boxes (I think they're intended for cake) with lids from Poundstretcher or Wilkos at £2-4 each for years - they do crack/break eventually but they're stackable and always replaceable. Our Dutch friends have huge low wide plastic buckets that they got from the market - we've seen them used in fish stalls at the market here, so if you can stomach it go ask at these (then scrub very clean!). Bear in mind you'll be wanting to cover prepped food until use, so lids are important, or clean tea towels that are large enough. You can also usually blag lots of large white empty mayo/sauce tubs from restaurants, and also once you start buying in bulk ingredients you can reuse tubs.

Large mixing bowls are useful, as well as some bits of Tupperware to keep smaller amounts of chopped veg or herbs in. Try to keep lids together with boxes! A few jugs are good for salad dressing or small amounts of sauces.

You'll also want at least two sturdy, large plastic boxes for washing up, especially in a field kitchen. We use proper strong plastic storage boxes with handles. If you can find a decent sink surface, this may be worth connecting up to the water supply where you're cooking, for washing up and/or handwash.

First Aid

You really should have a decent First Aid kit in a kitchen. You'll at least need a huge amount of plasters. For catering purposes, people use blue plasters, the idea is that if they come off and fall into food, they'll be easy to spot cos have you ever heard of blue food? The kit should contain the normal first aid stuff, plus things against burns, and bug bites and wasp stings if you're cooking outdoors. Keep it accessible, obvious and in its own separate space in your kitchen by the way – it's really shit if you're bleeding all over the place but you just can't find the bloody first aid kit that's buried underneath 25kg of couscous.

Fire safety stuff

A fire in a kitchen isn't uncommon, so you may want to invest in a fire extinguisher (a small one costs about £20 new at B&Q's or somewhere like that). A fire blanket is good too for potential fires in pans. Again, keep this stuff somewhere obvious and accessible.

Laundry

Teatowels are useful for holding hot things or covering food, but they aren't much use for drying - you'll just get through millions of them when drying 100 plates. It's much better to dry things in the air. Also, when used too long, teatowels are evil germ collectors. The same goes for handtowels. We actually end up using paper towels a lot for drying our hands, and for things that do need drying immediately, or to dry things well before putting in storage (because stacked wet plastic plates or tubs in storage will go disgusting). Big rolls of cheap blue roll are the stuff of food hygiene dreams.

Aprons are fun for not getting covered in food. The theory is that they're meant to protect the food from you! Somehow. I guess if you're all crusty and stuff (not like us of course). Make sure you collect dirty laundry, keep it separate and wash it regularly!!!

Tables

For serving, food prep, food storage, washing up, tea and coffee serving... Figure out how many you'll usually need. You can get sturdy tressle tables with folding legs e.g. from army surplus which are by far the best to use. If wood, you can sand them down and paint them with gloss paint to create wipe clean surfaces - they'll keep better too. Hard plastic tables with folding legs are good, but can be quite heavy, and expensive unless you find a bargain second hand. Wallpaper pasting tables just collapse - not recommended, except maybe to keep aprons on?

Marquee

If you're planning to cook outdoors most of the time, you might want to invest in your own marquee. A large, light one - white, or cream - is much, much nicer to cook in than the army-style dark green ones because it gets hot and steamy from the burners. We don't have one and always just ask the organisers of an event to provide us one, which they usually happily do.

NB on 3rd edition: We did eventually buy a marquee, one of those plastic-y garden party type ones which did seem to have a very sturdy frame, was easy to assemble, we didn't need a truck to transport and it seemed a good deal and we were really pleased with ourselves. However, at one event, SOME PEOPLE didn't strap it down to the ground properly and it blew away in the middle of cooking dinner, bounced straight across a field full of people and children and whatnot, and then the frame was weakened and it blew away a second time... and died... stupid thing.

Random other

We always also pack: stereo--batteries--music--gaffatape--adjustable spanner (to connect gas bottles) and other basic tools--string--masking tape (useful for labels/signs)--lighters ('long' metal ones are great for lighting scary powerful burners)--tinfoil and clingfilm—cashbox--marker pens--strong binbags--pegs to hang up aprons etc—spare jubilee clips and plumbing stuff--tons of washing up sponges and surface cloths, plus washing up liquid and antibacterial surface cleaner--dustpan and brush--a wheelbarrow to transport heavy food. We once saw a cool portable bin - I think it was from a garden centre and it folded down or pulled up into a wire/cloth bin, we want one.

Storage

If you're accumulating all this kitchen tat, you'll need somewhere to store it. You'll also need space to keep herbs/spices/dried leftovers off the ground and where rats or slugs won't eat it! A garage, a basement, a van, or a spare room will do. We started off with the big pans in our shed, and everything else under our beds or behind the sofa... In the end, thank fuck, we shared a garage for the big stuff and the basement of our social centre for the food.

PLANNING TO COOK AT AN EVENT

What follows is things you'll be needing to think about/sort out before you cook somewhere, and organise when you're cooking.

Where Will We Be Cooking?

There are so many settings you could be cooking in from your own kitchen at home to a field in the middle of nowhere. Wherever you are, find out as much as you can about where you will be cooking before an event. Questions to ask include:

Indoors kitchen: How much space is there? Is there safe storage space for food? Is there a sink or two in the kitchen? Is there a stone floor or sturdy, non-flammable surface you can set up a burner on? Where does rubbish go, is there recycling/composting? What kind of kitchen appliances are already there, or cleaning supplies like mop and bucket?

Mobile kitchen: Where will you be able to set up? Will your dodgy pasting table take the weight of what you're taking? Will there be a bin nearby or should you take one? Where can you take your rubbish after? Is there a tap nearby or do you need to bring water?

Outdoors event: Will the event organisers be supplying a space to cook in (e.g. marquee)? Will there be a water point next to the kitchen? Are there any other things on site you could use (pallets for food storage off the ground, electricity supply, straw bales or chairs to sit on, tables, bits of wood to make things out of, hosepipe, tilly lamps, fire extinguishers, ...)? What is the vehicle access like? What can you do with waste water? Where does the rubbish go?

We definitely prefer cooking outdoors - you don't end up with a slippery floor covered in food you need to constantly clean, we can set up our big burners without worrying about setting the floor on fire, make a wet mess washing up, and generally, it's nicer to be in a field than in a city!

Food/Menu

You can just show up and see what veg is cheap at the market and cook it, but you may prefer to make a plan. This should include a full menu, all ingredients, where you'll get them from, and how you will cook them.

This is where a good spreadsheet comes in handy (things scribbled on scraps of paper do the job too though). It'll include numbers expected, and notes on logistics, i.e. pans available, cooking times etc. The spreadsheet becomes our shopping list, and we also keep it in the kitchen for reference.

We usually divide up responsibilities for each meal on the day, instating one person as the 'cook' for each dish, who then nabs others to help them wash and chop veg or do other prep. For example, for a lunch with spaghetti, sauce, salad, tea and coffee, it'll look like this:

estimated 100 people (revise amounts if less or more people):

DISH	INGREDIENTS	WHO	HOW
Spaghetti	10k (2 boxes)	Tom	Pan 1
Sauce	*5kg onion, garlic, 5kg courgettes, 3kg red lentils, 10 large tins chopped toms and 5 tom puree, 1 large tin olives, basil, oregano, paprika, 1 bottle red wine,*	Dick	Pan 2
Salad	*10 mixed lettuces, a few red*	Harry	

	onions, tomatoes and cues, dressing with white wine vinegar and olive oil and fresh parsley,		
Tea and coffee		Tom	In Pan 1, after spaghetti
Serving	Setting up serving and finding volunteers to help	Harry	
Washing up	Setting up washing up area and finding volunteers	Dick	

To avoid serving vegan slop every day, it's good to vary textures, colours and tastes in your menu. It is also worth making the effort to serve a number of different dishes in one meal, e.g. a main dish, plus sides, salads, seeds... This means that even if someone is allergic to a dish or fussy about foods, they will hopefully still find something they like/can eat on their plate. It also means that even if you only have one large pan, you can up the quantities you are able to serve by making extra salads and sides.

If you know there will be a lot of kids, serve them first and make sure some of your dishes are kid-friendly. We sometimes just have some fallback baked beans, hummous, bread and carrot sticks or similar to offer to kids if they don't like our main offerings.

Make sure you have enough 'staples' for any event: oil, vinegar, lemon juice, mustard, salt and pepper, margarine, flour/cornflour (to thicken things last minute!), stock/boullion, tahini, vegan mayo, soy sauce, seeds, sugar...

Maintain a good supply of herbs and spices - best stored in sealable large jars packed together in a crate/box. Herbs and spices lose their taste over time, and do go off, so remember to keep the best before dates written down, and don't exceed them by too much.

We almost always forget something, or find we're running out of something, and need to do last minute shopping and send someone off to buy a few more things. Even after years we have been unable to avoid this. In fact, once we forgot all our herbs and spices and had to contend with making bland food the whole weekend.

Food Suppliers

You'll need to get your ingredients from somewhere, and if you're buying in bulk, there is absolutely no point going to a normal supermarket. You should be able to get discount bulk buying accounts with food suppliers. Even if you are just going to your local market to get veg, you should be able to negotiate bulk discounts - and a 25kg sack of potatoes will always work out cheaper than buying smaller amounts. You might also be able to blag some cheap/free things that are about to be chucked out.

We like to source food suppliers local to where we are cooking; sometimes event organisers or hosts have pointers. For organic suppliers, there's multiple online directories, and the Soil Association has useful links too. If you're on a limited budget or you're not fussed, search for 'wholesale vegetables' for the area and/or ask around for a nice farmer or where the local farmers or veg wholesale market is. If you're having to go with a bogstandard veg supplier; you can still apply some discerning criteria e.g. choosing seasonal foods and UK produce. Most producers will happily advise you on what's currently abundant, cheap and readily available! Sometimes this could mean breaking up your orders and getting just a whole load of courgettes from one farm, a bunch of lettuce from another and everything else from a wholesaler but despite the hassle at least you are supporting your local producer and partially cutting out the middlemen/women.

There are a few large wholefoods distributors that can provide you with staple goods – sacks of rice, soymilk etc. – that have all cornered particular geographical areas, in some way I've not quite understood but there's a list at the back of the main ones we have used.

Some companies will want trade references from other suppliers you've bought something off if they are unfamiliar with you (some will not care and just be happy to get large orders). Sometimes paid receipts will do. Another reason to keep records of who you've ordered from in the past – keep a folder with copies of your major invoices and receipts, also as a useful reference for the next time you are cooking in the area, or to compare prices year to year, or whether the amounts you ordered turned out correct, etc... And it appeals to those like me who like to hoard things!

Nearer the time, we will decide who sounds best/nicest of the suppliers we spoke to, and place our orders - best to give them at least a week's notice, and arrange for someone to be there (either ourselves, or someone involved in the event) to accept the orders and hand over payment. We usually end up with up to four deliveries: wholefood dried goods, vegetables, bread, and gas.

There's usually some items that are uneconomical to get from bulk suppliers, for example one jar of mustard, or one bottle of soy sauce. We just go to the shop for these bits and bring them along.

Cash and Carry

I.e. wholesale shops. There might be one in your area, and they're often full of over packaged stuff of not too great quality, but you might want to check them out anyway. You often need to register as a trading customer to access them, but you may be able to borrow someone else's card.

Skipped Stuff

One of the horrific statistics of modern society is the amount of perfectly edible food that is thrown away in Western societies – in the UK, about a third of what is grown for human consumption ends up in landfill! - in the face of poverty and hunger both within

Western societies and worldwide. We are greedy and wasteful, both in the production of our food and at the table. At every step of production and distribution – and in our ridiculously complex society there are a stupid amount of steps – good food ends up thrown away, so why not acquire and redistribute it?

If you decide to try and get food that's been chucked out to cook with, you'll need to be more flexible in your menu, and make sure the people you're feeding will be all right about the source of the food. A lot of restaurants,food shops both wholesale and retail and veg markets chuck loads of still decent food out every day, so try and figure when they chuck out what, or approach them saying you are a charity cooking group and would appreciate any leftovers to cook meals with for those in need, or whatever. Bear in mind you don't have to take everything they offer you – you may as well pick up the best stuff! You might end up securing a regular pick up deal; do try to keep to this schedule if you agree to it because you will lose your source of free food if you lunch it out too often or are constantly later than agreed. Commercial businesses need to pay for their waste disposal so in theory they may well be quite happy for someone to be reducing their waste bulk at no cost to them. Other blaggable businesses could include your local wholefood co-op or other 'right on' businesses. Even these will be producing food waste so you may as well check what they do with it...

Try and find the skips of food processing businesses or wholesale suppliers/markets, because they will be chucking out loads of stuff in bulk that isn't even out of date yet. And/or speak to your local FareShare or similar redistribution group and see if you can get stuff through them.

Bear in mind you're feeding other people, who may have more sensitive stomachs than you, and that you might be happy risking food poisoning yourself with something a bit dodgy, but maybe not 150 others... Wash all veg well before use. Avoid mouldy veg, the roots of the mould will have spread through the whole vegetable even if you cut off the obviously mouldy bit, and lots of people are allergic to mould. It's not advisable to use packaged food that's been opened (you might be fine eating it yourself but that's up to you). Take weather

27

conditions into account, for example, food that's been sat in a skip for a day in the hot sun is much more likely to be off!

Other Logistical Issues

Wherever you're cooking, put some thought into how you're setting up your kitchen so that it makes the cooking easy, things are to hand, and there's enough space to move past each other and you won't get in each other's way. If you can, make yourself a nice 'rest area' too. In the diagram you can see we generally try to separate the cooking area - off limits to non cooks - and the area open to the public.

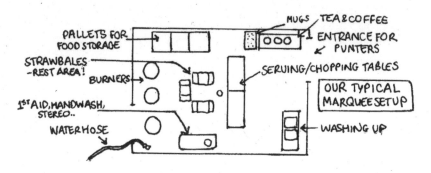

Food Storage while cooking

Try to organise your food storage in a way that makes sense, so that you can find things, and also so that it's all safely off the ground (not going soggy/attracting rats), covered (so bugs can't fly into the bags), or not liable to go off from heat. We sometimes use the van for additional food storage, e.g. dried goods and tins, if we're not expecting to use it too much during the time.

Prep

With numbers to feed from 50 upwards you will need to enlist extra chopping help – a meal for 150-200 people will need a couple tressle tables with 4-5 volunteers each on them doing prep, and you may want to stagger the prep for example get all the veg that needs cooking done first – and do these in the order you need them! - then clear up and do the salad veg in a second round. Once the prep is done and things are cooking you can dispose of your volunteers... get them onto the washing up or something and get them out of the way!

Washing vegetables

You'll need a few decent strong plastic boxes to wash veg in. Some scrubby sponges or brushes should be set aside just to use on veg (not to get mixed up with washing up sponges), and really muddy veg should maybe even be washed in one and rinsed in another box. Some veg doesn't really need washing: onions, garlic, tightly packed red and white cabbages, organic tomatoes, cucumbers, um, I might be missing out some really obvious ones here. Loose cabbages, lettuces, leeks and basically veg with 'folds' in should be sliced, torn or held apart while washing to get into every corner. Some salt in the washing water helps 'disinfect' veg, apparently. And some vinegar in lettuce water helps keep the lettuce crisp. A large salad spinner will help prevent soggy lettuce (and is good for washing herbs too!).

We have also now perfected the art of hosing down muddy potatoes and shaking off lettuces in a shopping trolley... Use a powerful hose with good water pressure and set it up in an area that can get wet, ideally on a hot day.

Handwash

A food hygiene requirement, and a sensible one really: have a separate handwash in the kitchen, that you don't use for anything else, with some decent liquid handwash soap (not perfumed - your food might start to taste of it). Make sure volunteers wash their hands before handling food – this especially includes people washing up. Use a container with a tap so you can wash your hands under running water and keep a wide plastic bowl or bucket underneath for the drainage.

Washing up

If you're cooking indoors and you have a decent big sink with two bowls, well, use this. Otherwise, set up a washing up area, either to be done by you or put out for people to do their own (but see notes on food hygiene). It will get messy so having it on a table/in a space of its own is best. Put pallets on the ground around it or straw/woodchips if you think it'll get muddy. One tub/box should have hot water - as hot as you can handle - with washing up liquid, and one should be used for rinsing. You may also want to add a third tub for pre-rinsing, as well as a bin for leftovers e.g. a sturdy box with a binbag in it. Have a few sponges and clothes and brushes. Put a crate next to the washing up to stack things up in to dry - having an extra pot for cutlery helps prevent chaos piles with everything falling to the floor... Change the water regularly.

Serving

You might just be serving as and when people come up and want stuff, but if you're serving a meal at a set time your serving needs to be organised a bit so it doesn't result in chaos and violence. Avoid looking like you're ready before you actually are cos people will start queuing up. You may want to do 'self service', but we definitely prefer serving, because it's quicker, we can make sure there's enough for everyone, and it's better from a food hygiene aspect too.

Clear a table to serve from, and give some thought to the potential 'flow of people' - e.g. they come in this way, give money/get tickets ticked here, then pass servers and take their plate here, then get to grab cutlery/salt/pepper, then can go get themselves a cup of tea or bread somewhere off to the side and not in the way, and/or leave out that way... will all that work? Have one person serving each part of the meal, or even set up sideways – see pic - and serve in two lines with two people serving each part of the meal on both sides. We also always have 1-2 cooks not involved in

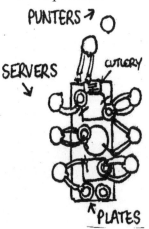

30

serving but hovering in the background ready to refill the serving containers.

We usually count out plates into stacks of 50 so that we can see at a glance how many people we have already served and whether our portions need to be bigger or smaller.

It's nice to let kids queue jump. If they'll eat your food at all, fussy things.

If you're using really big pans, ladle some food into not so huge pans to serve out of. Refill when needed, and reheat if necessary. Set up the serving so you're putting hot food on first, and salad/raw food last cos it's icky if it gets covered in cooked food. Personally I like the different servings on my plate to not touch but I have some kind of weird thing about it and I admit that not everyone else does...

Give people equal portions but try to have enough for seconds for the big eaters - make sure you've served all firsts before you call for seconds. We just let people help themselves to seconds, but you may end up with fistfights over the last veggie sausage.

Waste water

If you can re-use water you cooked veg in (this does not go for potatoes and most beans - it always goes scummy), for example in a sauce or soup, do so. Generally you will need to be tipping away a fair bit of water though, plus washing up water, so if you're indoors, make sure you've got a drain that can handle large amounts of water splashing through it all at once (and keep a floorcloth handy to wipe the floor after to avoid it getting slippery and dodgy). If there's an outdoor drain near the kitchen, use that.

If you're in a field, ask whoever's usually living there/using the site where a good spot near the kitchen would be to make a slosh pit. This means digging a hole in the ground you can empty dirty water into in the hope it'll drain away (some ground is not good for this). The deeper the hole the better, basically you want to hit a place it can drain into. Position pallets over and beside it, so you can stand over the hole and tip stuff in, or rinse things off with a hose over it etc. We need these to wash up our large pans over. Also ask if it's okay to just fling washing up water into a ditch or bush or wherever. But any water with traces of cooked food should really go into a slosh pit or somewhere far away - it will attract rats etc. if randomly tipped out by the side of the kitchen.

You may also want to look into setting up a greywater system for your field kitchen if you are in a place for any period of time, which can be a more or less elaborate construction that filters your waste water. Look it up on the internet if you're interested in this; a word of warning though that on really a large scale grewater systems can get overloaded and be really fucken gross. I have too many ick-memories of scraping out food waste gunked hemp sack lining ugh....

Rubbish

It's nearly impossible to not produce large amounts of rubbish. For consolation, you will still be producing less than if 100 individuals were all cooking for themselves! Find out what can be recycled where you're cooking; you'll generally have shedloads of compost (make sure you know whether the compost will be able to take citrus peelings, garlic/onion peelings, and cooked food), lots of cardboard packaging and boxes that your ingredients come in, and maybe tins and bottles depending on what you're using. People seem to like to have somewhere to scrape their food remains into, so set a compost box up next to the washing up. Make sure you don't leave food remains in the kitchen overnight when the kitchen's unattended but get it out of there - and not just in a binbag right outside - because it will attract rats.

A good way to avoid too much waste is also to put some effort into calculating how much food you will be needing! Of course sometimes you just don't know how many people will show up and eat, but the more of an idea you have the better.

We have cooked a couple times at gatherings at an animal sanctuary where we could feed the pigs, sheep and ponies our leftovers... now that was the best. I suspect that our cooks deliberately made too much food just to be able to watch the pigs lever sheep out of the way to eat it.

Dietary requirements

If you can, ask people to get in touch with you BEFORE an event to discuss any allergies/special dietary requirements. We do this a lot but hardly anyone responds, then we come cook somewhere and 10 people complain they can't eat this that or the other, AFTER we've cooked everything... Hopefully people do come up to you and you can look through your menu and see how you can accommodate them. If you have a few different parts of a meal, you may be able to give someone more of what they can eat and leave out what they can't. If you're using nuts in a meal, it's a good idea to leave them to be stirred in last minute so that any potential nut allergies can have some without. A lot of people seem to be going wheat free or gluten free these days, so bear this in mind when planning meals.

Wheat, barley, rye, bulgur and couscous all contain gluten; oats may be 'contaminated' with gluten but some claim not to be. Corn, rice, millet, quinoa and other grasses are gluten free. Also watch out for soy sauce (sneaky, sneaky soy sauce), which contains wheat – the superior taste of the wheat free equivalent tamari compensates a bit for the extra cost. If we're serving a wheat based meal we'll usually offer a wheat free alternative, and many meals are wheat free anyway, but we won't inflict gluten free products (e.g. pasta or breads) on everyone, partly cos they can cook badly (gluten free pasta clump anyone?) and partly due to cost.

FOOD HYGIENE

It's advisable for at least a few people in the group to do a food hygiene course. A community training organisation in your area might offer free accredited courses for community groups. You can also easily do them online – make sure they are City

and Guilds accredited – for as little as £15.

If you face a food hygiene inspection cooking at an event (something that has happened to us a few times - especially at events accessible and open to the public), showing a few food hygiene certificates will improve your chances - as well as cooking vegetarian or even better, vegan food - meat and dairy worry inspectors more. The things we have noticed food hygiene inspectors seem to be especially keen on are: notices displayed in kitchens re. food hygiene, temperature control systems, having a separate area for day clothes (jackets, bags etc), and cooks wearing aprons and tying back their hair.

Also, knowing about food hygiene isn't a bad thing if you are taking on the responsibility of feeding hundreds of people, and you don't want to make them ill. It's also not just important within the kitchen. If people aren't washing their hands properly after going to the toilet bad things happen and kitchens will get blamed, so it's worth feeling a bit responsible for general hygiene matters where you're cooking, especially if you're in a field. Check if there are handwashes by the loos, set up a handwash outside your kitchen people can use before they eat, and one by the washing up. Lots of people dipping their hands in lukewarm washing up water is an ideal ground for ick-germs to proliferate and spread! Use antibacterial handwash and not just some hippie shit.

A lot of food hygiene is common sense, but the main points are:

- **Wash your hands** *before handling food. Have a separate handwash basin, or bowl, with anti bacterial soap.*

- **Don't do gross stuff** *like pick your nose or sneeze into your hands, then carry on handling food.*

- *Don't use* **tea towels** *when they're soggy and manky - avoid them altogether, or wash them often. Don't use dishcloths until they disintegrate, change them frequently.*

- *Food needs to be kept at the* **right temperatures**. *Hot food should actually be hot when serving, i.e. over 70°C/160°F, cold food should have been stored, covered, in somewhere cold (under 5°C/40°F). Lukewarm food breeds bacteria* and bugs etc. Monitoring temperature is an important food hygiene requirement, so if you think you'll be inspected, you'll need thermometers in any fridges/freezers, and a probe thermometer to test cooked food (they come in a huge price range - a cheap one will do). You'll also need a book to log the temperatures in (cheap from catering supplies and useful cos it tells you exactly what you need to do).

- Don't leave food to be served sat around for too long, and keep it covered when not serving. If you are keeping prepped stuff for longer than a couple hours, it should be labelled with the date it was prepped. Leftovers should only be re-used if you can cool it all down properly and then re-heat it all again properly and it's not sat in the sun or exposed to contamination by animals or whatnot. This applies especially to rice, which may have spore-forming bacteria that survive cooking and rehatch and multiply in cooked rice left at room temperature.

- Store all food stuffs **off the ground** (even indoors). A pallet will do for this if you're outside. Don't leave packaged food uncovered/exposed.

- **Surfaces** used for food prep and serving should be wipe-clean, i.e. either gloss painted wood tables, hard plastic, stainless steel, or covered with a plastic tablecloth. And like, wipe them regularly.

- You should be **using utensils** when serving food (not serving with your hands, or letting people help themselves to food with their hands).

- Be aware of **Health and Safety** - i.e. don't block the paths you are using when cooking with boxes, leave knives on the edge of a table, walk around with knives pointing away from you, leave things hanging off precariously, leave exposed wiring, also make sure your gas lines etc are obvious and not in the way, etc. Another thing to consider is keeping the cooking area non-public/not accessible to everyone and their dog since random people traipsing through will get in the way, trip over your gas lines or discard their dirty jackets on your food storage or spill their beer into your dinner, and definitely piss you off very quickly. Oh yes. Keep the public OUT. Maybe your drunken non-helping friends too.

- In terms of equipment, plates and mugs shouldn't be excessively cracked and chipped. Opened bags of sugar/beans/herbs etc should be kept taped shut, or in Tupperware or jars with lids. You will also need thermometers for temperature *controls. Food Hygiene people also are really into signs saying such obvious things like: Now wash your hands, or which chopping board for which food, or No Smoking, or Germs Exist.*

FINANCES

Ooh the fun bit. If you're not a registered company, you won't really have to keep accounts (if you are - well, you'll have to keep proper accounts, and you'll need to go somewhere else for advice on that). But you will be handling money, and you'll probably be keen on not losing money.

In the UK, you can open a clubs and societies account at most building societies with two or more signatories although this has become harder in recent years. Choose a name for the account that doesn't sound too far off from what you're calling yourselves. We didn't want to open an account called 'Anarchist Teapot', so we opted for some entirely random harmless sounding name, and this has led to lots of unnecessary confusion. I think I'd call it 'Teapot' if we were doing it again.

When you set up, you will need a fair bit of cash - to get equipment, but also to pay for the ingredients upfront before you cook at an event (and eventually get the money back).

We usually budget for each event by itself. We take the expected numbers, and round that down (event organisers are almost always over optimistic, somehow). Then we figure out how much money we could expect to take. Then we divide that figure up into the different categories - wholefoods, veg, bread, gas, random extra shopping, transport, plus running costs if there are any. Usually we add up what we expect to be spending, then go, oh we need to cut that down. No olives for these people this time. Or we may find we're under the budget in which case people get more olives, and maybe even nuts.

This is an example of a budget for a weekend gathering, cooking for up to 250 people for 3 days. We'd assume some variation in numbers over the days.

Expected Income
100 people on Day 1 x £6 a day = £600
200 people on Day 2 x £6 a day = £1200
250 people on Day 3 x £6 a day = £1500
= £3300 available

Expected Outgoings
Dried food order: £1200
Bread: £100
Veg: £1000
Gas: £100
Transport: £200
Other (shop/equipment etc) £300
= £2900

Travelling to an event, make sure you have enough cash or cheques with you to pay for things upfront such as deliveries, petrol, last minute shopping. If you want to figure out whether you're losing money on an event or not, keep a written record of all money taken, and all money spent. Also take it into account whether you have leftovers at the end that will keep until your next event (keep a record of your leftovers to consider when you next order too).

We usually have one person 'in charge' of the money during an event, who takes and pays out money, and keeps the cash (you might well end up with bundles and bundles of cash... lock it up somewhere safe, and don't just keep it all in a bumbag and then get drunk and lose it... eh-hem).

There's different options for taking money. We'll often just do food by donations at one day events, or at demonstrations and the like. This can work out fine, and we cover our costs, but we find that cooking over a number of days, people stop giving you donations cos they spent all their money on beer. We also don't particularly like handling cash while serving food, fiddling for change etc., so we sell day meal tickets when we can, and have a 'ticket checker' in the dinner queue. This also helps us know in advance how many we're cooking for.

If you do kids' portions you should charge less for them. Bear in mind that some teenage kids eat more than a small horse though.

If we notice we've made a loss at an event, we'll appeal to the organisers and see if there's any spare cash generated from it floating about that they can stick toward the food. Or explain the situation and ask for donations before people leave. Or, if we recently have made a decent surplus on another event, or we'll be cooking at an event soon at which we can expect to make a surplus, we'll write off the loss. This has worked out okay in the long run for us, but maybe we're just lucky?

TOP TIPS – If you're lazy you can just read this bit.

Mass catering is all about having adequate equipment, being resourceful, and being organised. You can never have too many lists or too much kit.

Propane gas is more powerful than butane. Thin bottomed pans burn. Lift cooked things out of water with a spider/drainer rather than try to drain a massive pan.

Get volunteers to help you with veg prep and washing up.

Put a few different dishes including some salads on a plate, that way it won't look like vegan slop.

Food hygiene and health and safety are not unimportant. Always wash your hands before handling food.

Keep your cool and keep it fun. Cooking is awesome, it shouldn't be stressful. Don't forget to sit down and have breaks too, don't martyr yourself, and make sure you enjoy the process of creating delicious food for the masses.

RECIPES

Mass catering is obviously different than cooking a meal for yourself and a friend. Also, unfortunately, it doesn't always work to just take a recipe for 4 portions and times it by 20/30/80. Or some things that sound great on paper just become slop when scaled up, or far too expensive, or logistically impossible.

Before you decide on what to cook, look at what equipment you have, how much time you'll have for prep, what veg is currently seasonal, or what kind of ingredients you may be able to get cheaper in bulk. Also try to imagine it in a very large pan that needs stirring all the time (this might well put you off some very thick sauces...).

Try recipes out at home first, maybe for a bunch of friends or something, before you buy 10kg tofu to make it on a large scale.

For ideas on cooking times, generally bear in mind that a large pan of water will take fucken ages to get to the boil. Especially if you've got a crappy burner. You'll get to know your equipment over time, and how long things will take, but before you know this, calculate at least 3 hours to prepare a meal for 150-300, and get water onto the boil as soon as you feasibly can. If you have a spare pan, it might be good to get water boiling in it to add to another pan later in which you've started cooking. For example, potatoes usually boil in 20 minutes. But 50kg potatoes will take much longer - first you need to bring a huge pan of water to the boil, then the actual cooking will take longer too, so it'll be more like 1 1/2 hours altogether.

I don't really want to prescribe amounts here for herbs and spices. Add spices generously, but bit by bit, and taste test as much as you can. Other things that can 'add flavour' that you might want to experiment with include: marmite/yeast extract/tamari, mustard (good in lots of soups), stock powder, thickening the whole thing with some cornflour mixed to a paste with water (add while boiling) or other thickening tactics, wine, sugar (kind of like a flavour enhancer - but beware of using too much and just making it sweet), fresh herbs, concentrated apple juice, bay leaves, tomato puree...

A good way of testing what something needs is to get out a small bowl, mix in what you're considering adding and then tasting it - before you just dump a kilo of something into the whole thing.

We usually end up with 6 people standing round the big pan 5 minutes before we should be serving arguing over what else the sauce needs...

You may need to be flexible if you end up with leftovers that need using up. This means either unused leftover veg, or prepared food that's okay to keep - either kept cool, or used very soon and reheated well. Things that won't keep seem to be curries, dressed salads, and anything that keeps the heat too well or involves rice. Leftovers — as long as not dubious from a food hygiene perspective - can often be used to bulk out what you're cooking (shh we obviously never do that).

Stirring/burning things

Large quantities of food in a pan will burn much, much easier than what you're used to, due to weight. Try to use pans with smooth heavy bottoms for anything that's not just water/really liquidy. Any time you start frying, be there stirring, always right down from the bottom up and evenly all around. Turn down the heat as soon as things start
sizzling, and turn up again only when you add liquid, which you should do as soon as things start sticking on the bottom - if you can anticipate it, right before that happens is best. Until it gets boiling, you'll need to carry on stirring at least occasionally (also depending on how thick it is), your food might be sat at the bottom and start to burn. Once something's vigorously boiling, you'll need to stir a lot less. If the bad thing does happen and it starts to burn, swear a lot, and stop scraping

the bottom because you'll mix the burnt bits throughout the food and it will all just taste burnt. If it's nearly ready, just turn it off, or if you can transfer it to a new pan, do that, but leave out the burnt bit. Lentils are an exception, if they start sticking, turn it off and leave it for a few minutes, they will magically unstick then you can start cooking them again with a bit of extra liquid.

If a recipe calls for veg and pulses to be cooked in a sauce, or if that's how you usually do it, we'd recommend cooking the veg and definitely the pulses separately in boiling water (stirring once in a while!), then draining and adding them to the sauce. It will take less time to cook, and your sauce won't be as heavy and as likely to burn.

Take turns stirring if you can, it can be tiring and hot, and you don't want to slack on it, cos burnt stuff is a bastard. And washing up burnt pans is also a bastard. Get soapy water in as soon as you can and leave it to soak, clean as much out as you can then get the burnt bits with a wire scourer, trying to avoid scratching up your pan too much which will lead to more potential burning.

Terms used in recipes

fry: usually just mean gently frying veg in some oil while stirring with enough oil to cover the bottom of the pan. Always fry as long as you can i.e. as long as the veg isn't sticking to the bottom, or going brown - this brings out flavour.

steam: cooking in a covered pan with the bare minimum of water.
Tbsp = tablespoon. **Tsp** = teaspoon.

41

AMOUNTS NEEDED PER PERSON

Muesli: 50g per person/1 lb per 10 people per day
Soymilk: 0.2l per person per day. Or 1 pint to 20 cups of tea.
Bread: just under 100g/0.2lb per person per day, 20 large (800g/nearly 2lbs) loaves will feed about 180 people at one meal
Sugar: ca. 1kg/2.2 lbs per 100 people per day for teas and coffees
Margerine: ca. 1kg/2.2 lbs per 100 people per day
Grains: 50-80g/2-3.5oz per person per meal
Couscous/bulgur: 5kg/11 lbs will do 60-80 people per meal
Pasta: 100g/3.5oz per person per meal
Dried beans: 50-70g/3oz per person per meal
Main dish: up to 0.4l/ 2 cups/ 2/5 quart per person per meal
Soup: ½ pint/0.3l/1.2 cups per person
Veg in a main meal: 250g/1/2 lb per person per meal (e.g. 150g/5oz potatoes plus 100g/3.5oz carrots per person)
Tomato puree: 35x 200g/7oz double concentrate tubes for a sauce for 200 or 4 large size catering tins (usually 900g/2lbs) for 100.
Lettuce: 1 tightly packed lettuce for 12 portions of green salad, about 10 for other normal size lettuces
Cabbage: 50g per person/1 lb for 10 for a cabbage salad or side dish
Cucumber: 1 cucumber for a cucumber salad for 6-8 people (less if just one ingredient)
Salads: For a salad buffet or meal based on salads, offer 1.5 portions per person in total (i.e. 3 different salads = ½ portion per person)
Vegan sausages: 10kg/22 lbs sosmix for ca 400 medium sausages
Bouillion/stock: about one large tin of stock powder (900g/2 lbs) for a soup for 200-250
Dressing: 1 litre/1 quart vinaigrette dressing for a salad for 100 people
Fruit: if budget allows or we've been asked to, we'll have fruit with lunch or dinner, usually asking people to just take one piece. In the UK, apples often come in 18kg/ 40 lbs boxes (100-150 pieces), Bananas also 18kg/40 lbs (average - 120 pieces), oranges 15kg/33 lbs (average - 65 pieces)

Hot Drinks

People exhausted from talking, organising, fun and games with the police, or just from life do appreciate a hot drink. Despite many political reservations regarding the global trade of black tea and coffee beans we loves it so we makes it. It's one of those products where the choice of source can actually mean a lot so do source your supplies well.

You can either set up a self service area or serve people hot drinks; generally self service works okay if you occasionally send someone round to tidy up and check the water's still hot.

At large scale events, we make tea and coffee in the kitchen and keep it hot in insulated urns. Basically, we use a big pan to boil up loads of water (which you'll also want for other things e.g. washing up), then ladle water into insulated urns with a big tea bag or through a coffee filter. The drinks will stay hot for quite a while. We made our own giant teabags by sewing them out of muslin (not too thick, fine or coarse), and we made a giant coffee filter to fit in the top of an urn out of a wire coat hanger and muslin. We use one pack of 125g/5oz loose breakfast tea for a large urn of black tea, up to 2 packets of 227g or 250g/8oz coffee for a full urn, and a large handful of loose herbal tea. We leave normal tea in the urn for about 10-15 minutes and herbal teas longer. Remember to check that the spout is shut when you start pouring water in! If the spout is leaky, it probably just needs tightening.

If you're using an electric or gas water boiler and doing self service, you can either just slum it and offer instant coffee, or you need to figure out a way of making coffee. Lots of cafetieres (which do use up a lot of coffee, and need a handy place to be cleaned), or a filter into a large coffee airpot are possibilities.

For medium-scale events, a simple filter coffee machine, the type that has a jug and can have another jug ready on top, is probably your best option. The standard catering use 'Bravilor' or 'Buffalo' ones are about £150-£200 new but keep an eye out for second hand ones.

The best water temperature for making coffee is at 88-93°C/190-

199°F, for black tea the water should be boiling (100°C/212°F), and green tea should be made with water at about 80°C/176°F.

Bear in mind that on a typical ring burner or water boiler, 5 litres/1.3 gallons of water from cold takes about 16 minutes to boil. 5 litres/1.3 gallons added to an already boiling boiler drops the temperature to 83°C/181°F and takes about 12 minutes to get back to boiling.

Breakfast

We usually do a self service breakfast. A selection of different cereals with milk and sugar put out is nice - e.g. a muesli, a crunchy muesli, cornflakes, plus dried fruit or fresh fruit. Some cereal mixes and cornflakes are not vegan, also make sure you label which ones contain gluten or nuts. Bread, set out on boards with breadknives, margarine, jams, peanut butter, marmite, homemade spreads are nice too. If you can put out a toaster, people will appreciate it. And of course, teas and coffee should be put out too.

If you have the facility to do this, people will love you if you fry them veggie sausages, mushrooms, tomatoes, cook scrambled tofu, and heat up baked beans for them. If you can be arsed. Cash and carries usually have large tins of baked beans or you can get organic baked beans in large tins, there's one brand that are oddly spicy though.

Scrambled tofu

Ingredients: onion, garlic, firm tofu (100g/3.5oz per person), salt and pepper
Optional: chives, turmeric, nutritional yeast, soy sauce

Fry a bit of onion, some garlic if you like, and then add tofu you've squeezed the water out of and mashed up with a fork, plus salt and pepper, and maybe some herbs like chives. Adding a small bit of turmeric will make it go yellow and resemble scrambled eggs. Also nice to add is some nutritional yeast (Engevita) and/or soysauce/tamari.

Bean Spread

Ingredients: cooked beans, olive oil, lemon juice, salt and pepper
Optional: onion, garlic, herbs, carrot or other veg

Good for using up leftover beans. Mash them up with some liquid, a bit of fresh lemon juice and a dash of olive oil, and mix in whatever you like: some fried finely chopped onion, garlic, herbs, salt and pepper, grated carrot, other finely chopped veg, either raw or fried (with the onions).

Yeast Spread

Ingredients: onion, garlic, fresh bakers' yeast, salt and pepper, parsley

A basic, easy spread involves fresh bakers yeast. fry a fair bit of onion, and a bit of garlic. Then crumble the fresh bakers yeast (one packet to a small onion) and add it to the pan, along with some salt and pepper, and lots of chopped parsley, stirring all the time. It will go all gooey. This one won't keep for very long so use as soon as possible.

Hummous

Ingredients: chickpeas, salt, tahini, lemon juice, garlic, pepper, olive oil
Optional: onion, fresh herbs

Much, much easier made with a blender - just chuck all the ingredients in and blend, adding more water if it needs it- but you can also mash it by hand or turn the cooked chickpeas through a mincer.

For 100 portions, soak (overnight), drain, and cook 9kg/ 20lbs chickpeas in enough water to cover plus a bit. Simmer for at least an hour. Leave to cool before you mix the other ingredients in. Then get a big mixing bowl, and mash chickpeas with up to 2 handfuls of salt, 3kg/6.5lbs tahini, up to a litre of lemon juice - fresher is nicer, but you will need to juice fuckloads of lemons - 2-3 bulbs of garlic, minced, some pepper, and up to 400ml/about 2 cups of olive oil. Add water gradually as you're mashing to end up with a decent consistency. Some finely chopped onion or fresh herbs can be nice too, or use butterbeans to make 'bummous'.

'Fake mincemeat spread'
Ingredients: ricecakes, onions, garlic, black olives, marmite/yeast extract, oil, tomato puree, herb salt, salt and pepper

This is a weird German recipe but it works well and makes for an interesting sandwich or roll filling. To make enough for 15, grind 8 ricecakes, either by hitting them a lot, or in a food processor (that works better). Mix with a bit of warm water til it's all stuck together. Chop 2 small onions finely, mince 2 cloves of garlic, chop 10-12 black olives, then mix with the ricecakes, adding 3-4 teaspoons marmite/yeast extract, 2 tablespoons oil, 2 tablespoons tomato puree, herb salt, and salt and pepper.

Porridge

Use rolled porridge oats, and mix in 2 1/2 times liquid (volume wise) - either water, soymilk, or a combination, plus a bit of salt. When well mixed, heat it up, stirring all the while, and simmer for about 5 minutes. Offer milk, cinnamon, sugar or golden syrup with it. On a very large scale, heat the liquid first, then stir it in to the porridge and cover and leave to stand for 5-10 minutes. The pan will be an arse to wash up--make sure you soak it immediately.

Soymilk

Oh the joys of making your own soymilk... It does make sense, because it avoids all the excessive packaging of one litre packets of soymilk, it can be hard to actually obtain 120 litres/30 gallons of soymilk, is cheaper, and generally more economical. You will need a spare pan to use for over an hour though, and the grinding of the beans might take quite a while... We've stayed up half the night making soymilk and have given up making our own.

1kg/2.2lbs dried soybeans will make about 5-7 litres/1.3-1.8 gallons of soymilk. Soak the beans overnight, then grind or mince them, either by hand in a mincer, or--much better--in an electrical mincer, or even a food processor. Add them to about the amount of boiling water your beans should yield in soymilk, and boil for about half an hour. When it comes to the boil, it might all go crazy so keep an eye on it, and you may need to quickly add some cold water. Strain through a large colander or similar item lined with muslin and cool as well as you can.

After straining, you'll be left with lots of ground beans. Rampenplan call this stuff Okara (I have no idea if they made up this name or it's real?) and it is then used as the magic bulking out ingredient. You can make burgers from it, use it in soups and sauces, etc.

Fresh soymilk will keep for less than a day in hot weather, a bit longer if you have the luxury of refrigeration. If not, keep it in an insulated urn if you can. We've made it the night before and it has then been okay for breakfast and lunch. It goes off if there's a storm, for some reason.

Pasta

Amount: usually about 100g per person.

Cooking pasta on a large scale can potentially turn into one big solid mushy lump, so first of all, boil up a shit ton of water and add salt. Get ready by opening all the packets you're using, and throw them all in when it's really boiling – put the lid back on the pan and try to get it back to the boil as soon as possible. Then, as soon as they're 'al dente' i.e. not soft but edible, turn the burner off and start scooping the pasta out as quickly as possible with a large slotted spoon/spider into a separate container. You'll need someone at hand stirring oil (and more salt if you want) into it, to prevent it from sticking, and/or rinse the pasta with cold water while you drain it to stop it cooking further and to wash all the starch off.

Hopefully it doesn't turn into one big gooey lump then. The shell shaped pasta, as well as the tube pasta, basically any pasta that potentially traps hot water inside it, can be tricky to use.

Ideas for pasta:

Bolognese Sauce
Ingredients: onion, garlic, oil, chopped tomatoes, tomato puree, soy mince or lentils, oregano and basil, sugar, salt and pepper
Optional: celery, carrots, courgettes, peppers, red wine, thyme, marjoram, paprika, parsley

for 200: fry up to 10kg/22lbs chopped onion with enough oil (5mm/0.2" is a good amount) to cover the bottom of the pan, add lots of minced garlic after a while (about 6 bulbs), and maybe some celery (not more than 5 bunches - it gets overwhelming), carrots, courgettes, peppers.... all chopped fairly finely. Keep sweating over a low heat as long as you can - stirring well!

As soon as it starts sticking be ready with chopped tomatoes - if you're using big 2.5kg/5lbs tins you'll need about 8-10. Add veg mince – ca. 5kg/11lbs (dried weight) of the MINCE, not the chunks – or red or brown lentils, up to 8kg - at this point too. Add liquid - water or red wine, mmh - if needed to just about cover the veg and mince and make stirring without burning possible, but make sure you don't add too much. Mix in some tomato puree to thicken it up, 4-6kg/9-13lbs.

Add herbs like oregano and basil (it can take a LOT of both of these), some thyme/marjoram if you like, paprika, salt, pepper, and sugar - a bit of sugar's good to add to tomato stuff cos it takes off their sourness.

Bring this to a boil then turn down and cook at least 30 minutes, til done, add more herbs and fresh herbs like a bit of parsley (not too much), basil, oregano, if you have them, toward the end.

Veg Tomato Sauce
Ingredients: onion, garlic, oil, chopped tomatoes, tomato puree, vegetables, oregano and basil, sugar, salt and pepper
Optional: cooked beans

for 200: Kind of the same as the above, but with more veg instead of mince. Use the calculation of 250g/1/2lb veg per person for this. Use veg like chopped onion, celery, carrot, quartered

mushrooms, sliced peppers, broccoli separated into bits with the stalks chopped up finer, even root veg like chopped parsnip, sweet potato, squash, potatoes. If you want to use things like spring greens or spinach, add them later on when you have the whole sauce boiling. You can also use some beans in this - less than 8kg, and use 5-10kg/11-22lbs less veg, and either cook soaked beans separately and add toward the end, or use tinned beans - soaked beans will take ages to cook in the sauce.

Creamy Vegetable Sauce 1
Ingredients: onion, garlic, oil, flour, stock, soymilk, bay leaves, salt and pepper
Optional: celery, carrot, fresh herbs, nutmeg, nuts

for 100: fry 5kg/11lbs onion in a fair bit of oil, and add say 5 bulbs garlic, and a bit of other finely chopped veg you decide to use - e.g. celery/carrot.

The following needs a lot of attention, so, attention! Slowly add about a third to half of a bag of flour and mix it in immediately so that it starts going all gooey down in your pan. Then have some stock ready - made separately with boiled water - to add bit by bit, alternating with some soymilk (ideally, both stock and soymilk will be warm. Don't boil the soymilk, just heat it gently). Keep stirring, and stop adding liquid if it's getting too thin.

Bring to the boil, and you may be able to add some more liquid then. Add about 10 bay leaves, some salt and pepper, and maybe some herbs, and a bit of nutmeg is nice.

Then, you could either be steaming some veg in a separate pan and adding it towards the end, or adding veg to the sauce to cook in it. Some nuts are nice in this too, like chopped cashews or hazelnuts.

Creamy Vegetable Sauce 2

Ingredients: spinach, garlic, tofu, basil, onion, mushrooms, flour, soymilk/stock, nutmeg, salt and pepper

for 100: Cook a whole load of spinach - 5-6 large bags of frozen spinach or up to 4kg/9lbs shredded fresh (you'll need to spend a lot of time washing the spinach though). Steam it with as little as water as won't burn, and until just done, then drain and mix in 4-5 bulbs chopped garlic.

Add it to a large bowl and mash it with a fork and/or masher/anything that'll mash, with 5-8kg/11-17lbs tofu and as much basil as you can afford - at least 4 big bunches. If you have a food processor, do it in that.

Then fry 5kg/11lbs chopped onion, adding up to 5 more bulbs of chopped garlic, 2kg/4.5lbs quartered mushrooms, and make a roux again (like above) with flour adding soymilk/stock and nutmeg. Mix in the tofu/spinach mash when done, taste test for salt and pepper and nutmeg, and serve over pasta.

Olive oil and garlic

Ingredients: olive oil, onion, garlic, salt and pepper, fresh herbs, black olives, capers
Optional: chillis

This needs a LOT of olive oil to be tasty, so it could become quite expensive for over 100 people, but it's very easy to make. It's basically slowly cooking a little bit of chopped onion, but mostly garlic in a whole load of olive oil, then mixing this into pasta with salt, pepper, fresh herbs like basil, chopped black olives and capers. You can also add in some minced fresh chillis.

Pesto

Ingredients: fresh basil or a mix of herbs, walnuts/cashew nuts, sunflower seeds, olive oil, salt and pepper.

Best made with a food processor. Lotsa fresh basil, toasted nuts, sunflower seeds, other nuts/seeds.., olive oil, salt and pepper and go whizz.

You can add a bit more oil bit by bit if you like, while it's going. Other fresh herbs are nice too, like parsley, fennel, rocket, mixed herbs... This is one to experiment with – you can make pesto out of pretty much anything for example wild greens like ransoms/wild garlic (don't add extra garlic in that case!!). Worth it if you can afford all that olive oil.

Genovese

Ingredients: new potatoes, penne or fusilli pasta, olive oil, salt and pepper, green beans, pesto, basil

for 100: This involves cooking things separately, so only really good for 100 or less on a decent burner with a few rings, while boiling the pasta water on a separate stronger burner if available.

Cook 5kg/11lbs small new potatoes until just done. Scoop out, and cool, then chop into cubes. Cook 6-7kg/13-15lbs penne or fusilli until just about done, scoop out and drain, mixing in olive oil and salt and pepper. Steam 6-7kg/13-15lbs green beans cut into 5cm/2" lengths (frozen ones are ok), drain. Mix all together with up to a kilo of pesto, garnish with basil.

Pasta bakes

Pasta bakes are possible if you aren't cooking for too many, and you have a big oven. You can usually fit four to six large (about 40cmx20cm/ 1'6"x8") baking trays in a large oven - with each baking tray yielding about 16 portions. Don't start stacking trays on top of each other, it just doesn't work, cos the heat goes down then. There's loads of recipes about for these, so I'm just giving you my favourite one:

Aubergine and Tomato pasta bake

Ingredients: onion, garlic, basil, oil, aubergines, pepper, chopped tomatoes, sugar, oregano, pasta, tomato puree, stock, salt
Optional: black olives

for 50: fry 8 large chopped

onions (ca. 2kg/4.5lbs), then add 4 bulbs of garlic, and two handfuls of dried basil. If you have a lid, cover this for a while, stirring occasionally. Cut up to 8 large aubergines lengthwise into quarters and slice, add them to the onion along with 10 sliced peppers, and 3 large (2.5kg/5lbs) tins of chopped tomatoes - or a mix of tins and fresh tomatoes. Cook for a while, add a dash of sugar and some oregano (less than a handful) if you wish. Separately, cook 1.5-2kg/3-4.5lbs pasta twists (e.g. fusilli) until just about done. Mix in to the sauce, along with some tomato puree (about 2x900g/2lbs) and a bit of stock, taste for salt needed. You can add some black pitted olives if you like. Bake at 200 degrees/gas 6 for about 1/2 hour.

Grains/The Stodge Part of a Meal

We often use couscous or bulghur as a grain side dish as it's pisseasy to make; our meals often consist of a 'sauce'/main dish/stew served with a grain or potatoes, and a couple of salads.

Couscous or bulghur

All you need is a pan with a lid and some hot water, but no extra burner, to cook these. Unfortunately people who are wheat intolerant or allergic are unhappy with this. If you can avoid it don't put too much of either in a pan to soak at a time, because the top ends up crushing the bottom and it goes all mushy (we use the army Dixie pans, and do about 4kg/6.5-9lbs at a time). Before pouring water on, you can mix in some dried herbs, spices, sultanas, boullion, olive oil, tinned chickpeas, lemon juice... oil will contribute to a decent grade of fluffiness. Pour water on until it's completely covered the grains with about a centimetre or more over, stir through and get a lid on, and leave it, stirring occasionally, for 5-15 minutes and checking if it's too dry and needing more water.

NB: We once made Teapot cook Top Trumps and Couscous Fluffiness was a category.

Rice

Amount: ca. 80g/3oz per person. It can be hard to get right - i.e. it's easily overcooked, burnt, and you end up with a pan that's a bastard to clean. Brown long grain rice is the easiest to not fuck up. Again, boil plenty of water (more than you'll need), cook it and before it's too soft, start scooping it out, draining well. You can add a bit of salt when it's boiling to help it along, or other spices either before cooking, fried up separate and mixed in, or mixed in when draining - cooked rice can easily taste of nothing but hot water.

Wholewheat, buckwheat, barley, rye, millet

These are all things we hardly ever cook, but hey, could be good. They all take a bit longer to cook than other grains.

Quinoa

Quinoa is a popular health food that's fairly expensive so we don't use it much. Apparently you boil and cook it for about 15 minutes, then leave the lid on and steam off the heat for another 5.

Boiled Potatoes/Mash

About 250g/1/2lb or a bit more per person. They're both very good instead of a grain with some dishes. Use a floury variety that's good for mashing. Boil up plenty of water, wash your spuds well (if well washed and with brown bits cut out you don't really need to peel them - peeling spuds is Bourgeois). Chop into small chunks for mash, large chunks to boil. You can be experimental with your mash and use a mix of root veg, just make sure you're adding them to the water in order of cooking time. Again, watch for when they're just about done, and scoop out quickly into a separate container, with someone there mixing in some margarine, salt, pepper, chopped herbs, ... If mashing, well, have fun, it does get there eventually. Try to use more marge than soy milk, unless you can heat up the soy milk before mixing it in (it cools it down).

Soups

Soups are great. They are usually filling, have lots of good nutrition in them, and they're not so hard to make - we often do soups for lunch, served with decent bread, because we usually have less time to do lunch compared to dinner, and we can also save ourselves washing up lots of pans... Experiment with soup recipes you find. These are ones we often use. frying veg at the start for as long as you can on low heat really gets flavour into the soup. Adding some 'garnish' when serving instantly makes it look nicer, e.g. chopped herbs (parsley/coriander/ chives) or sprigs (rosemary/ thyme/mint), toasted seeds, a 'swirl' of vegan yoghurt or cream, a dusting of paprika, croutons...

A lot of soup recipes call for the soup to be liquidised. This is quite hard to do properly with 50 litres+ of soup, unless you have a giant industrial blender which costs about £500. We often use soup recipes that don't need to be finely pureed to be nice.

Emergency thickening

Mix up some cornflour with water to a paste, or 2 tbsp arrowroot with 1 ½ tbsp water, or equal amounts of flour and marge crumbled together, and stir into a boiling soup to help it thicken a bit. If the soup's too thin and you still have enough time, adding some red lentils, if compatible, will absorb a lot of water (they'll cook in 20 minutes).

Stock

If you have a spare pan, it's worth making your own stock. Check out the many stock recipes in books, or re-use water you've cooked veg in and add some things like fresh herbs/bay leaves/marmite, or boil up a bunch of water with a few whole veg in it like carrots, lots of onions, garlic cloves, celery, celeriac, a bunch of fresh herbs (e.g. 'bouquet garni' with thyme, bayleaves, parsley), cook for as long as you can, then scoop out all that after a bit or strain the whole thing. You'll need about 20-25 litres/5- 6.5 gallons for 100 people.

If you're buying stock cubes or bouillon, go for an organic one - so much better, and no mono sodium glutamate/E numbers etc. Some aren't vegan, and some have nuts in them - avoid if you can, cos it fucks the whole soup up for nut allergic people. We sometimes use the 1kg/2.2lbs pots of Marigold bouillon, but some aren't vegan and those that are often have nuts in them. We like Vecon which you can get in 1kg/2.2lbs pots, it's a darker, saltier stock, and a bit more 'meaty'. Stock cubes are a really big pain when you have to use 30 little individually wrapped cubes. Remember that bouillon and stock will have salt in them, so don't overdo it when adding more salt – taste test.

All Soup Recipes for 100
Potato Based Soup

Ingredients: onion, garlic, oil, salt and pepper, stock, potatoes, fresh herbs, other vegetables

There's loads of variations for this one. fry up to 8kg/17.5lbs chopped onions, add 5-6 bulbs minced garlic (optional). Have the heat fairly low, and enough oil in, then add altogether up to 20kg/44lbs chopped veg, mostly potato. You can also use combinations of: carrot, finely chopped celery, sliced leeks, shredded greens, chopped turnip/parsnip/other root veg, chopped herbs.

For leek and potato soup, use 15kg/33lbs potato and 5kg/11lbs leeks.
For watercress and/or spinach soup, use 16-18kg/35-40lbs potatoes, and add 8-10 large bunches/bags of greens when the soup's boiled and the spuds are nearly done.

Add water or stock (also use a bit of white wine if you're posh! mmh), enough to just cover the veg. You can still add more later if it's too thick and nearly burning, but you might not be able to thicken it, so be careful. Bring to the boil, then simmer until the potato starts breaking down when you're stirring. Stir a lot, pressing the potatoes up against the sides of the pan to break them down. Carry on cooking even after it's done, so it breaks down as much as possible. Taste test adding salt and pepper, and maybe some Dijon or wholegrain mustard and fresh chopped herbs.

Lentil Soup

Ingredients: onion, celery, garlic, oil, salt and pepper, stock, red lentils, bay leaves, herbs, lemon juice
Optional: carrot, chopped tomatoes, potatoes, parsley, cumin, miso

Fry up to 10kg/22lbs chopped onion, 2-3 finely chopped bunches of celery and/or a bit of finely chopped carrot, and even a few potatoes (chopped small – sweet potato is also really nice to use) to help thicken the soup later.

Add 3.5 kg/7.7lbs red lentils, ca.

20 litres/5 gallons of water or stock, and later, when the lentils are cooked, up to 10kg/22lbs chopped tomatoes (4 large 2.5kg/5lbs tins).

Alternatively, use up to 6kg/13lbs red lentils, about 25 litres/6.5 gallons water or stock (enough to cover).

Add bay leaves and maybe herbs like thyme, basil, rosemary, sage. Bring back to the boil, simmer for 20-30 minutes, longer if it needs to break down more. Stir a lot.

Add salt, pepper, and up to 1/3 litre/1 ½ cups of lemon juice at the end (more if you're using real lemons) and maybe some parsley. You can also add a more interesting flavour to it if you fry up some very finely chopped onion with garlic and cumin, separately, then mix this in. Don't put in too many herbs though if you're doing this.

Another alternative is lentil and miso soup - cook the soup with some grated carrot in it, then add 2-3 large packs of miso bit by bit when it's boiled (mix in well) and take it off the heat.

German Lentil Soup

Ingredients: onion, garlic, celery, carrot, potatoes, brown or green lentils, bay leaves, marjoram, stock, salt and pepper
Optional: veggies sausages, parsley, fresh marjoram

Fry up to 10kg/22lbs chopped onion, 2-3 finely chopped bunches of celery, then add some garlic (4-5 bulbs), up to 4kg/9lbs of chopped carrot and up to 8kg/18lbs potato chunks, (do you see a pattern emerging in these soups...?).

Stir well and get ca. 25 litres/6.5 gallons of water in before it starts to stick, along with up to 6kg/13lbs brown or green lentils, a few bay leaves, marjoram, and a stronger stock like Vecon unless you're using homemade stock. Bring to the boil and then simmer.

It's really nice, if you can, to separately fry up a bunch of veggie sausages (50/60 will do for a soup for 100 if they're fairly big), then chop them up and stir into the soup at the end. Taste test with salt and pepper. Sprinkle with a bit of fresh parsley (not more than 3 bunches) and some fresh marjoram if you can get it.

Carrot and coriander

Ingredients: onion, garlic, celery, oil, ground coriander and ginger, carrots, stock, fresh coriander, salt and pepper

Well, kind of the same again: fry up to 10kg/22lbs chopped onion, celery, garlic - if you like, you can add a little bit of ground coriander or ginger too - then add 15-20kg/33-44lbs chopped carrots (maybe some potatoes too) and water/stock and bring to the boil. Use a lighter stock for this one.

Simmer, stir a lot so it breaks down, and then add salt, pepper and 4-5 bunches of chopped coriander with the toughest of the stalks taken off (bit of a fiddly job).

You can also add some grated carrot to thicken it more. It can be nice to mix in a bit of soy cream at the end, but don't let it boil after adding. Or serve the soup with a fancy 'swirl' of soy cream.

Minestrone

Ingredients: beans, onion, garlic, potato, carrot, celery, chopped tomatoes, stock, bay leaves, fresh herbs, macaroni, salt and pepper

Optional: cabbage leaves/greens/dark kale/courgettes, green beans

Soak 5-6kg/11-13lbs haricot or cannelini or borlotti beans overnight. Bring a large pan of water to the boil, and cook the drained soaked beans until done.

Fry 8kg/17.5lbs chopped onion, then add 6-8 kg/13-17.5lbs diced potato, 6-8kg/13-17.5lbs diced carrot, 2-3 bunches of sliced celery, other veg if you like such as some chopped cabbage leaves or greens or chopped courgettes, and 5 bulbs minced garlic.

Fry until just before starting to stick, at least 5 minutes, then add 10kg/22lbs chopped tomatoes - fresh is nice, but tins are okay too, or half and half. Also add about 20 litres/5 gallons water or stock, and some fresh herbs like bay leaves, parsley stalks, thyme sprigs, rosemary sprigs (if you want to tie them together like a 'bouquet garni' DON'T use plastic string, or rubber bands, or anything else that'll melt!). If you want you can also add some green beans here - if using frozen ones, add later on with the beans.

Bring to the boil and simmer til veg is cooked. Now add the

beans, and pasta - use 3-5 kg/6-11lbs macaroni or other small pasta. It'll cook pretty quickly once it's boiling again, so check it often. Taste test with salt, pepper, and a bit of sugar if it's too tomato-sour, and stir in some fresh basil if you have.

Veg and Coconut Soup

Ingredients: onion, root vegetables, oil, marjoram, ground ginger, cinnamon, spring onion, stock, flaked almonds, chillis, sugar, creamed coconut, fresh coriander, salt and pepper

A chunky root veg soup with creamed coconut stirred in toward the end is lovely.

Fry 7kg/15.5lbs chopped onion, add up to 20kg/44lbs cubed veg - any combination of potatoes, carrots, sweet potato, swede, pumpkin, squash, turnip, and add one or two large handfuls of marjoram, a handful each of ground ginger and cinnamon.

Fry as long as you can, then add 7-8 bunches of spring onion, chopped (both the green and white bits), 30 litres/8

gallons stock (or until the veg is covered, but not much higher than that), 200g/7oz flaked almonds or more if you have, some finely chopped fresh chilis - say 10-12 small ones, and a large handful sugar.

Bring to the boil then simmer til veg is done. Grate or generally chop up 2.5-3kg/5-6lbs creamed coconut (a bastard job), stir in until dissolved, season to taste then serve with lots of fresh coriander (6-10 bunches).

Sweetcorn and Coconut Soup

Ingredients: onion, garlic, red peppers, carrots, root ginger, sweetcorn, creamed coconut, salt and pepper
Optional: chillis

This is easy if you have access to frozen sweetcorn, less viable otherwise.

Fry about 8kg/7.5lbs finely chopped onion for a few minutes, then add a 6kg/13lbs box of finely chopped red peppers, maybe a few kilos of finely diced carrots, and up to 5 bulbs of minced garlic.

Stir for a few minutes, then add 1 large root of grated ginger, or a

58

large handful of powdered ginger, and if you want a spicier soup, add about 10 finely chopped red chilis (don't touch your eyes!!). Add about 20 litres/ 5 gallons water and bring to the boil.

Add 5-6kg/11-13lbs frozen sweetcorn, and 2.5-3kg/5-6lbs chopped creamed coconut (wholefood distributors will often sell creamed coconut in large blocks), and salt and pepper. Bring back to a gentle boil and then simmer for a little while longer until the coconut is dissolved and the sweetcorn is cooked. Season to taste.

Courgette and Tarragon Soup

Ingredients: onion, celery, carrot, tarragon fresh and dried, courgettes, stock, salt and pepper

A nice one for the summer when courgettes are abundant and everyone and their dog donates you their surplus courgettes from their allotments.

Fry up to 10kg/22lbs chopped onion with 2-3 finely chopped bunches of celery and a bit of finely chopped carrot, and maybe a handful of dried tarragon. Then add up to 15kg/33lbs courgettes chopped into chunks. fry as long as you can, then add 20-30 litres/ 5-8 gallons stock or until the veg's covered. Boil, then simmer until cooked. If you can, scoop up some (up to half of it) out and mash or blend, then return to the pan. Add lots of fresh tarragon, season to taste and serve.

Other nice soups

Here are some other nice soup ideas easily done in bulk; make them up yourself or look out for the recipes in recipe books: Veg (especially squash) and peanut soup, Broccoli/cauliflower soup with flaked almonds garnish, Corn chowder, Butterbean and tomato, a dhal type soup, Lentil and veg soup, broad bean/pea and mint... Or try chilled soups like Gazpacho or Cucumber if you have some chilling facilities available. They're nice in summer.

Soups that suck to make in bulk are any of the ones that involve roasting veg first - the veg shrinks away and you need absolutely tons. Mushroom soup can be done for up to 40, beyond that gets complicated and pricy. Borscht - beetroot soup - is lovely but you will spend 7 hours peeling beetroots. Same goes for Jerusalem artichokes. Clear soups are unsatisfying as a meal in themselves, and miso soups get pretty expensive.

Croutons

You can either make them in a flat frying pan or in the oven. Use slices of day old bread, cut off crusts, and then cut into cubes. Fry in a bit of olive oil or a mix of olive oil and sunflower on medium heat in a frying pan, turning all the times with a spatula, and sprinkle with things like herb salt or other herbs, or fry a few bits of garlic in the oil first to get a garlic flavour. Or grease a flat baking sheet and put in the oven on medium heat, turn them a couple times and keep a close eye on them.

More Main Dishes and Sauces

These are some of our staple dishes all suitable for cooking with basic large scale equipment for large numbers. Occasionally, and depending on the scale of the event, equipment available, and the budget, we'll vary from this, e.g. making bakes, buffets, fancy things, new recipes....

Curries

There's lots of different curries you can make (check out any Indian cookbook for inspiration, or try Thai ones). They can have a base of tomato, just spices and stock, or coconut, and have any combination of veg, fruit (apples!), pulses and nuts in them. You can use those Pataks curry pastes (some of which aren't vegan - check ingredients) or your own combination of spices.

The general idea is that you fry onion first with spices (or spice paste), in LOTS of oil. Basically, I cretinously define curry as food with lots of oil and spices. Choose from ground cumin, coriander, mustard seeds, crushed cardamom pods, turmeric, ground or fresh ginger, minced garlic, fenugreek (kinda stinky), chilli, cinnamon, garam masala, other spice mixes.

Anyway, you then add veg, frying for as long as you still can, then water or chopped tomatoes, thickening with creamed coconut, chopped nuts (ground almonds are nice in a korma), cornflour, or tomato puree. If you're adding pulses, soak and cook them separately and mix in toward the end. Use about 40-50g/1.4-1.8oz pulses per person, depending on how much veg you're using.

We like to serve 2 contrasting currys (e.g. tomato and aubergine, with a korma-style one with cauliflower and green beans) and/or a dhal, with couscous or rice, plus a couple of salads or raita like cucumber with mint, and/or tomato and red onion, chopped onion with herbs, and pickles. At some cash and carrys and in Asian shops you can get huge jars of pickles and chutney, which are well worth it! 3-4 large jars usually are enough for 300 people unless they're especially greedy.

Dhal

Ingredients: peas or lentils, onion, turmeric, whole spices, garlic, cumin, ground coriander, cumin seeds, black mustard seeds, oil, fresh coriander or lemon juice or coconut cream.

Nice served with curry, dhal is made either out of yellow split peas, red lentils, or other lentils.

Bring lentils or soaked yellow split peas up to the boil; the ratio should be about 1 part lentils to 2 parts water.

Add chopped onion, turmeric, any whole spices e.g. bay leaves, cinnamon sticks, cloves, cardamom. Stir well and regularly. If it starts sticking to the bottom, turn the heat off, let it sit a bit then get back on.

When cooked, fry lots of garlic and cumin, ground coriander, cumin seeds, and/or black mustard seeds separately in oil, and mix this in, including the oil. Adding some fresh chopped coriander, or a bit of fresh lemon juice, is nice too, or a smallish amount of coconut cream (to a red lentil one), let this dissolve on the heat.

Potato or Bean Provencale

Ingredients: potatoes or beans, onion, garlic, red wine, chopped tomatoes, tomato puree, herbs, salt, pepper, sugar, pitted olives
Optional: courgette/carrot/celery/aubergine/peppers

It's basically potatoes, or beans and some veg, in a tomato/red wine/olive sauce. We usually serve it with garlic bread and a green salad.

Get a large pan of water boiling (for the potatoes or the beans).

Fry a lot of onion (amounts for 200: ca. 10kg/22lbs) , add lots of garlic (a large plate full when chopped), and if you like, some finely chopped courgette (not more than 5kg/11lbs) or carrot (same), or sliced and quartered aubergine (same), or sliced peppers (same) or a combination. Sliced peppers are especially nice with the beans, use a bit more for this (6-8kg/13-17.5lbs).

Add red wine (2-3 bottles, depending on how much the cooks want to spare), bring to the boil and leave boiling for a few minutes. This makes the actual alcohol evaporate, but leaves the nice wine taste in. Then add chopped tomatoes (4-5 2.5kg/5lbs tins), and simmer a bit, then start stirring in lots of tomato puree (4-6kg/9-13lbs).Add any combination of marjoram, thyme, basil, oregano, rosemary, plus salt, pepper and sugar (not too much). Cook until dark red, stirring all the time.

Add pitted black olives (3x 2kg/4.4lbs tins - usually available from wholefoods distributors) near the end.

Cook cannelini beans (10-12kg/22-25lbs) - you can also use a mix of beans, e.g. butter beans, cannelini, and some flageolet - cook together according to cooking times - OR potatoes, chopped into large ish chunks, separately. Scoop out when done - if the beans boiled up all frothy, rinse them a bit before adding - and mix in to the sauce. Taste again for salt before serving.

Greek Beans

Ingredients: haricot beans, olive oil, garlic, stock, bay leaves, fresh oregano, tomato puree, lemon juice, red onions, pitted black olives, salt and pepper, sugar.

for 200: Soak 10kg/22 lbs haricot beans overnight and cook until done.

Gently cook beans in lots of olive oil or a mix of olive and sunflower with a lot of garlic (15 bulbs or so) stirring well, for a few minutes.

Add up to 30 litres/8 gallons stock (until covered), bay leaves, some sprigs of fresh oregano (tie them together with non-plastic string to fish them out after), 4-5 large tins of tomato puree (it shouldn't be too red altogether), lots of lemon juice - use both fresh and bottled - enough to give you a good whiff of lemon when you sniff it - and some chopped red onion (about 5kg/11lbs).

Simmer, stirring a lot, for as long as you can, up to an hour is good.

Then add 2-4kg/5-10lbs halved black olives and salt and pepper.

This is also good cold. Serve with French stick and a green salad for a simple meal.

Nuts and Beans

Ingredients: black eye beans, oil, onion, garlic, chopped tomatoes, tomato puree, chopped nuts, parsley, salt, pepper, sugar.

for 250: Soak 12kg/26.5lbs black eye beans overnight in nearly twice the volume of water. Scoop out and boil up in enough water to easily cover, when they're done, scoop out, sprinkle a bit of salt over, and mash as much as you can. You're not making a puree or proper mash, you just want to be breaking it down a bit. Try to keep this warm, or time it so it's done just before the rest of the meal is.

Meanwhile, fry 15kg/33lbs chopped onions, add 10 bulbs of garlic, then 20-25 large (2.5kg/5lbs) tins chopped tomatoes, and 3 large (900g/2lbs) tins tomato puree.

Bring to the boil. When it's cooked a bit, add 8kg/17.5lbs chopped mixed nuts, 8 or more chopped bunches of parsley, salt, pepper, a handful of sugar or a bit more, and the mashed up beans. This mixture will be a fucker to stir now, so don't even try to cook it much longer.

This is nice served with boiled new potatoes with some marge and parsley stirred in, or rice, and salads.

Aubergine and Lentil Stew

Ingredients: aubergines, brown lentils, chopped dates, onions, garlic, red chilli, oil, ground cumin, cinnamon, a bit of smoked paprika, salt, pepper, soy yoghurt and parsley

for 50: Soak about 2kg lentils for a bit, then boil for 20 mins. Drain and keep the liquid. Cut about 6kg aubergines into cubes and roast in an oven or fry in oil turning often until soft and put aside. Cook 3kg onion, a couple of bulbs of garlic and a couple of chillis until soft, stir in cumin and cinnamon, and 350g chopped dates. Add te lentils and drained liquid to cover, and simmer for 25mins. Garnish with yoghurt and parsley if you got!

Chilli

Ingredients: kidney beans, onion, chillis, paprika, cumin, coriander, cayenne pepper, cinnamon, oregano and basil, peppers, chopped tomatoes, tomato puree, carrot, sugar, salt and pepper, chocolate or cocoa powder.

for 100: You may well have your own way of making it - everyone seems to! But here's how I do it; others in the Teapot make it different...

Soak 5kg/11lbs kidney and/or black beans overnight. Scoop out, and bring to the boil in plenty of fresh water, turn down and cook until done - scoop out while rinsing if you can, and keep ready.

Fry 5-6kg/11-13lbs chopped onion, after a bit, add 8-10 finely chopped chilis (and don't touch your eyes when you chop the chilis! ow!), and spices: small handfuls of paprika, cumin, a bit less coriander, less cayenne pepper, and cinnamon. Herbs like oregano and basil are good too. Stir well, and watch it doesn't stick.

Add 6kg/13lbs sliced mixed peppers before this happens. Be ready with opened tins of chopped tomatoes - 4-5 large (2.5kg/5lbs) tins. If you have fresh tomatoes, use half the amount of tins, and add about 4kg/9lbs chopped fresh tomatoes.

Keep stirring, and add 2-3 large (900g/2lbs) tins tomato puree. Add 2-3kg grated carrot. Simmer until carrots are soft.

Add the beans toward the end, a bit of sugar, taste test for salt and pepper. If you have some dark chocolate (1-2 large bars), break it up or grate it, and add it while it's still cooking - mmmh. Or at least add a bit of cocoa powder.

You can serve chilli just with rice, or also as a roll-it-yourself burrito, ie on a tortilla wrap with a few toppings (rice, guacamole, salsa, a sour cream alternative, some jalapenos – you can get big tins at wholesalers), and a few tortilla crisps on the side (get big bags from the shop or wholefoods).

Apple Hotpot
Ingredients: butter beans, oil, onion, apples, salt and pepper, turmeric, mixed spice, cinnamon

for 50: This sounds weird but it's very tasty and simple. It needs a lot of stirring to start with so we haven't actually ever made it for over 100 people.

Soak 4.5kg/10lbs butterbeans overnight, cook until done and when draining, keep the water. fry about 10-15 sliced onions for a few minutes, then add the same amount of sliced apples and a good handful each of turmeric, mixed spice, and cinnamon. Stir until well mixed through and the onions are cooking, then add the cooked beans and some of the liquid-- until not quite covered. Stir through and simmer for another 15-20 minutes, add salt and pepper and serve with crusty or garlic bread. Also nice served with vegan yoghurt mixed with chopped dried apricot (3x500ml/ pots plus ca. 150g/5oz apricot).

Cooking Pulses

If you need to hurry up cooking dried pulses, add a whole chunk of margarine to the beans when boiling. Make sure beans boil vigorously for at least 10 minutes to break down the toxins in some of them. Add some bicarbonate of soda to the cooking water if you want to counter the farting effects. We don't do this, we enjoy making everyone fart....

Goulash
Ingredients: onion, oil, carrots, parsnips, soya chunks or veggie burgers, paprika, chopped tomatoes, tomato puree, caraway seeds, stock, potatoes, salt and pepper, soya cream, parsley

for 100: Fry 4-5kg/9-11lbs chopped onion, then add about 6kg/13lbs carrot chunks, and 5kg/11lbs peeled and cubed parsnips until they start to brown.

Add ca. 6kg/13lbs veg soya chunks (get organic ones if you can), OR use the equivalent amount of fried up veggie burgers chopped into chunks. Also add a large handful paprika, 2-3 large (2.5kg/5lbs) tins chopped tomatoes and/or some fresh chopped tomatoes, 1-2 large tins of tomato puree, and half the amount of the paprika of caraway seeds.

Heat gently, then add some stock (up to 10 litres/2.5 gallons - much less if you've used cubed burgers) and about 5kg/11lbs diced potatoes. Bring to the boil, then simmer on a low heat for about half an hour until the veg chunks are done.

Season with salt and pepper, then stir in up to 3 litres/3 quarts warmed soya cream and a bit of parsley (1-2 chopped bunches, unless you can 'garnish' the servings with this), heat through but don't boil again. Nice with rice, cooked new potatoes, mash, or chunky bread, and salads.

Satay Sauce

Ingredients: onion, garlic, oil, celery or spring onion, chillis, ginger, chopped tomatoes, peanut butter, lime/lemon juice, salt and pepper, vegetables
Optional: creamed coconut or coconut milk

Fry onions, garlic, maybe a bit of celery and/or spring onion, fresh chopped chillis, lots of fresh finely chopped ginger for a while.

Then add a bit of water or stock, some chopped tinned tomatoes (not too many), and slowly add lots of peanut butter stirring all the while, until you have a sauce that's still creamy and stirrable but thick enough to not run - try to bring to the boil but if it starts sticking, you're going to have to turn it off. Add some lime or lemon juice and salt and pepper. You can also stir in some creamed coconut or coconut milk at the end.

Cook some veg separately like shredded cabbage, carrots, other root veg, broccoli... Then mix in the sauce (taste test again - it may need more salt).

Beans and Rice

Ingredients: onion, garlic, oil, beans, long grain brown rice, coriander or cumin, pepper, vegetables

This is from the Food not Bombs cookbook: fry onion and garlic, add water and beans - kidney/pinto/black, one part beans to two parts rice to five parts water.

Add one teaspoon of salt for each gallon of water and let the beans boil for 45 minutes or less if you soaked them beforehand (advisable with most beans).

Add long grain brown rice, half a cup of coriander or cumin per gallon, some pepper, and any vegetables if you like, e.g. carrots, onions, dried tomatoes. Cover the pan and bring to the boil again.

Stir up from the bottom, then lower heat and continue boiling until all the water is absorbed, or ca. 45 minutes. Don't stir more than once after the rice is in.

Sausages and Burgers

Meals like bangers and mash, with veg like cabbage stew or peas and gravy or cider sauce, or burgers with mash, or in buns with salads, go down really well, but be warned - frying burgers and bangers for hundreds of people will make you go crazy after a while. Use a griddle, brushed with oil, or a wide, flat wok/frying pan on a burner with lots of oil - it'll be greasy but it'll cook a lot better.

For **sausages**, we use vegan sosmix - a 10kg/22lbs sack makes about 400 medium sized sausages. We mix up a quarter or so of the sack at a time, then add some finely chopped onion, maybe some minced garlic, herbs both dried and fresh (finely chopped parsley for example), a bit of paprika, and whatever else we can think of. Then add cold water stirring the whole while, until it's stuck together but thoroughly moist and stir-able. Leave it to stand for at least 10 minutes.

Then start shaping into sausages - this is fucken tedious. Have some flat trays, Tupperware lids, or chopping boards ready to stack them up on. Have a bowl of water next to you to rinse your hands with when they get covered in sosmix. If it's too moist and is just falling apart, mix in some flour. If it's too dry add a bit more water (bit by bit – a tiny amount can make quite a difference!) and leave to stand for a bit again. Fry in batches and keep warm in an oven, or serve as you go.

For **burgers**, either use a burgermix with your own additions, same as with sosmix (chopped fresh coriander is really nice in burgers), maybe stretched with things like some cooked pulses (lentils, or other mashed ones), really finely chopped or grated veg like courgette or carrot - experiment at home! Otherwise, there's a lot of ways of making nice veggie burgers with any kind of pulse, nuts, grains, or vegetables as the main ingredient mixed with some cooked onion, vegetables and flavourings and some breadcrumbs or oats. About 1.25kg/3lbs lentils, plus 2.5kg/6lbs breadcrumbs will make about 100 burgers. To help

bind burgermix without eggs, use some grated raw potato or soya flour. There's a gazillion burger recipes - again, experiment at home! Coating homemade veggie burgers with breadcrumbs then frying them gives them a nice crispy edge.

Using a burger shaper - with clingfilm - takes a bit of practise but can make it a lot easier, especially if you've not got a whole army of burger shapers. And you end up with evenly sized burgers.

You might want to do burgers as part of a meal, but if you want to serve it as a bun, with relishes/ketchup/lettuce and other salad/mayo maybe you might want to just give people a burger and a bun, and put out the other things so people can help themselves - make sure you have enough of everything though, and put things out with tongs/serving spoons.

Other meal ideas

sweet and sour veg, stir fries (for under 100), tagines, bean stews, chow mein style noodles mixed with fried veg in a bit of sauce, stroganof, ratatouille on grains, kidney beans and veg in a coconut sauce with lime and coriander, soymince and veg stewed in gravy sauce on mash, rice pilafs (for under 50), caponata (sour aubergine stew) ...

Things that *don't* work well or need to be adapted are very heavy sauces or sauces in which veg and beans that need to cook in a heavy sauce (unless you can cook the sauce and veg/beans separately); paellas and risottos seem to be difficult to make for over 30 people; things involving a roux, i.e. a creamy sauce with flour - if you want to try it, make a roux separately then mix in to the finished meal.

Oven dishes

If you have access to a decent oven and you can either bake things and keep them warm, or you're feeding less than about 80, your repertoire expands massively. I'm not going to include a lot of recipes in here but here are things that work scaled up and you can easily find recipes for, and we've done before for 30-80:

jacket potatoes with fillings, roast veg (though doing a full Sunday roast for anything over 30 is a right pain), lasagne, shepherds pie, puff pastry pies

(e.g. 'steak' soychunk and ale pies, with a pastry crust), enchiladas, patatas bravas (roast potatoes with a spicy tomato sauce)...

Serving Bread

Just a few notes on bread here. You might put out bread with breakfast, and/or with soups, or for sandwiches. Find a nice bakery that does organic bread if that's what you'd like, and try and get the largest loaves you can find (usually 800g/2lbs). If you can get them sliced and bagged up, there are advantages, but also some more waste. You might want to ask for half of the bread to be bagged up so it keeps better. Fresh bread will be okay, stored in bakers' trays in a not too hot place for a few days (possibly up to 3), but if you're cooking over nearly a week, it's best to try and arrange two or three deliveries of bread, unless you've got some means of freezing loaves.

We usually put bread out, with serrated knives to slice them on a few wooden chopping boards, with margarine and spreads. If illness is getting a foothold you may want to avoid everyone handling bread and pre-slice it.

Serve them with tongs or in napkins.

A bread table needs looking after a bit - it gets really messy! And leaving open jam jars outside attracts bugs and wasps - so make sure they're not left there opened for ages.

Rolls, for example with soups, are nice too - just make sure you've got enough. It somehow fosters resentment if 120 people get rolls and the last 10 just get slices of bread... you might end up with a bread riot.

Garlic Bread

A tasty addition to meals like pasta, stews, etc. but you will need an oven, though it doesn't need to be huge cos it's fairly quick and you can do it in batches. An easy way to do it is to take a long baguette, chop it into 5 equal bits, then halve each bit lengthways and spread with garlic margarine (margarine mixed with crushed garlic, maybe some chopped herbs, and a dash of olive oil for taste and to help it spread). You need about 500g/a bit more than a pound of margarine for 50-70 portions. Layer into baking trays and bake for up to 15 minutes, keep warm in a covered container sat on top of the oven. This way, you end up with 10 pretty equal portions out of one baguette, and it's much less fiddly serving this than garlic bread sliced through that needs breaking into pieces while serving, possibly resulting in uneven portions which again can cause resentment (garlic bread riot).

Salads

Salads can help make your meal more interesting and more nutritious, without needing more pans/causing logistical issues. We often serve up a salad meal for lunch consisting of a few different salads, including at least one substantial one like a grain salad, a dip, and some breads or tortilla crisps.

Here are just some ideas for salads - get inspired by whatever's in season and available, and don't be afraid to use fruit, nuts, seeds, beans, cooked veg, fresh herbs etc.

*green mixed salad, with different lettuces, red onion slices, cress, avocado chunks, cucumber, seeds, sweetcorn, grated carrot, ...

*cannelini beans with vegan yoghurt, garlic, cucumber, mint and parsley

*grated carrot and sultanas, with orange dressing

*coleslaw - shredded cabbage of any type, grated carrot, sultanas, apples, kale, seeds, mayo — there's a lot of tasty variations...

*mixed bean salad with red onion, avocado chunks, sweetcorn, apple...

*tomato and red onion and fresh basil

*cooked green bean or broccoli salad with garlic and flaked almonds

*'chef's salad' with cooked potato, kidney beans, and any other veg like cress, grated carrot, chopped celery, in a mayonnaise/yoghurt dressing

*shredded Chinese cabbage, grated carrot, beansprouts mixed with sesame and olive oil, soysauce, pepper, ginger and some sugar

*tabbouleh - bulghur wheat (or finely chopped raw cauliflower), lots of fresh parsley and mint, tomatoes and cucumbers, chickpeas

*waldorf salad - celery, apple, seedless grapes, walnuts, cauliflower florets, mayonnaise

*'salad nicoise' - cooked French bean and potatoes, tomatoes in

vinaigrette with finely chopped black olives and capers

*grain salads – quinoa, couscous or barley with roast veg, red onion, herbs, lemon and olive oil

*brown rice and brown lentil salad – with a bit of red onion, parsley, tamari and maybe some seeds and/or seaweed

*potato salad – with onion, vegan mayo, parsley, maybe some gherkins and/or peas (use salad/waxy new potatoes and take care to not overcook!). Leave to cool before mixing the rest of the ingredients in.

Salad ingredients to pick and mix:
shred/finely slice: broccoli, brussel sprouts, cabbage, cauliflower, endive, leeks, kale, lettuce, peppers, runner beans, watercress

slice: banana, cooked beetroot or carrot, chicory, cucumber, fennel, orange, pears, tomatoes, red onion

chop: apple, celery, avocado, nuts, herbs, mooli, pineapple, radishes, spring onions (use both white and green parts).

grate: raw beetroot (it's a bastard to peel though, so don't get over ambitious), brussel sprouts, carrot, celeriac, onion, kohlrabi

other stuff: cress, nuts, raisins, sultanas, dessiccated coconut, grapes, beansprouts, alfalfa, edible flowers, cooked beans or lentils, potatoes, roasted vegetables, toasted seeds, croutons...

Lettuce

There's lots of different kinds of lettuces so when ordering veg, talk to the supplier about what they've got at the moment, and get a nice mix. It's a shame to resort to boring watery iceberg lettuces. Wash fresh lettuces well - some vinegar in the water will help crisp them up, as well as drawing out pesticides. If they're organic, watch out for baby slugs hidden in the folds... Dry well. A large, decent salad spinner is a great investment for this, otherwise shake a handful of leaves a lot and cover yourself in water. You can also have lots of fun washing and shaking lettuce in a shopping trolley with a hose.

Salad dressings

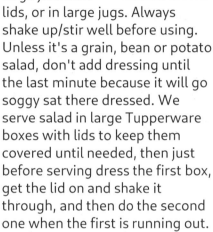

Make dressings in large jars with lids, or in large jugs. Always shake up/stir well before using. Unless it's a grain, bean or potato salad, don't add dressing until the last minute because it will go soggy sat there dressed. We serve salad in large Tupperware boxes with lids to keep them covered until needed, then just before serving dress the first box, get the lid on and shake it through, and then do the second one when the first is running out.

Vinaigrette: You won't need exactly 10 times as much as you use at home for 10 times the amount of people - basically it goes further in bulk. We'll make about 1 litre/quart of dressing for 50-100 portions, and about 3 litres/quarts for 250. But we're also kinda stingy.

Use 1 part vinegar/lemon juice to 3-5 parts oil. Mix vinegar (cider, white wine, red wine, or balsamic) and/or lemon juice with salt, pepper, and anything else you'd like to add: fresh or dried herbs, mustard (wholegrain or Dijon), minced garlic, a bit of tahini, apple or orange juice, a bit of vegan mayo or soy cream (make sure you whisk it in), miso or engevita/yeast flakes and soy sauce. Add olive oil, veg oil, some other oil or a mix slowly, whisking away while you're doing this. If you're using a jar with a lid, screw lid on and shake it all through. If you have a stick blender, use it to make it emulsify properly and go nice and creamy.

Vegan mayo: You can easily make your own vegan mayo, with a decent food processor or stick blender. For nearly a litre, liquidise 50-100ml/1/2 cup lemon juice, 400ml/2 cups soymilk and a dollop of mustard, then slowly drizzle about 700ml/ 3 cups vegetable or olive oil into it while liquidising, until it's thickening. Add salt and pepper, and garlic, fresh or dried herbs, paprika... if you like.

Mayonnaise dressing for 100-200 (depending on how much you want to smother the salad): Get a 3kg/6.5lbs tub of vegan mayo or use homemade mayo. Put into a big bowl, and mix in 1-2 500g/17.5oz pots of vegan yoghurt - this makes it altogether less heavy. Add a bit of lemon juice slowly, mixing vigorously the whole time, plus salt, pepper, and maybe chopped fresh herbs (parsley, dill, mint, tarragon) or minced garlic. You might also want to mix in a bit of veg oil, if it's getting too lemon-y. Make sure you wash out and reuse that mayo tub, they're handy for herbs and spices.

Vegan Salad Cream (for about half a pint): Mix 150ml/2/3 cup undiluted concentrated soymilk (comes in half litre cartons) with 150ml/2/3 cup oil, 5 teaspoons brown sugar, and some salt. Beat in 150ml/2/3 cup lemon juice with a whisk. You can add spices like paprika, ginger, curry spices, or fresh herbs.

Sesame dressing: Mix sesame oil mixed with veg oil, tamari, and rice wine vinegar in similar proportions to vinaigrette. Then add a bit of miso, dijon mustard and pepper, and grated garlic or ginger or herbs if you like.

Vegan Caesar dressing: To make half a litre, blend 200ml/nearly a cup of lemon juice, 2 cloves garlic, 2 teaspoons capers, 1 tbsp Dijon mustard, 2 teaspoons engevita (nutritional yeast flakes), a pinch of pepper, and 100ml/1/2 cup olive oil in a food processor. Gradually add 200ml/ nearly a cup of veg oil and salt.

Fruity dressing (to make about a litre): Whisk 600ml/2 ½ cups orange juice, 100ml/ ½ cup lemon juice, 150ml/2/3 cup apple juice concentrate, 3 teaspoons grated fresh ginger and 1 tsp caraway seeds.

Side Dishes

The more different things people have on a plate, the happier they seem to be. Or they at least think it's a more interesting meal. If you just can't always do this logistically, you can think about making more than one salad, or adding simple sides. Maybe you are able to get the main meal ready, and make a quick side on the freed up burner, then serve it all up.

Nuts: A garnish of chopped salted peanuts is nice with stirfries and similar, walnuts, brazilnuts or hazelnuts are nice with almost anything, cashews are nice with curries or stirfries.

Toasted seeds: get a large wok or frying pan hot, don't use oil, and bung in seeds like sunflower or pumpkin. Stir a lot over a slow heat until they start going brown - you can also mix in some sesame seeds toward the end, but turn it off as soon as they all start popping and flying out.

Mixing in some light soysauce or tamari when you take it off the heat is especially nice. Spread them out in a tray rather than a bowl - they end up weighing down on each other and sticking if stacked too high. We use 5kg/11lbs for 250-300.

Vegetable side dishes: like steamed greens or broccoli (though they have a tendency to go cold within seconds), corn on the cob, simple stirfries like shredded broccoli and nuts or greens with sesame, roast veg if you have an oven.

Peas: steam frozen ones over whatever you're boiling, in a large colander. Use a medium sized bag for up to 20 portions.

Boiled carrots: I like to cut them into sticks rather than rounds to resemble school dinner less and because I have a round carrot phobia; use plenty margarine, and mix in some golden syrup - not too much - and sesame seeds in at the end. Use 5kg/11lbs for 100 as a side.

Stewed cabbage/greens: finely shredded and stewed with a bit of onion in plenty margarine, you can add some garlic maybe, salt, lots of pepper and seeds like sesame, cumin, or caraway. You can also mix in some soy cream at the end if at hand. An alternative flavouring would be mixing in some soy sauce and sesame seeds at the end, or sesame oil if you got. Use 1 medium cabbage for 20 small portions, or 1 tightly packed cabbage i.e. white or red for 30.

French or runner beans: steam frozen ones in a colander over whatever's boiling, then mix in margarine, lots of minced garlic, salt, pepper, and maybe some fresh chopped parsley. It's even better if you can cook the garlic in the margarine before mixing it in.

Baked Beans: go well with things like bangers and mash - get some large tins from the cash and carry and heat - add some of your own flavourings if you like. Organic beans are of course nicer, the only thing is that they're usually only available in small tins.

Stewed red cabbage with wine: shred red cabbage. fry red onions (1 to each cabbage), and add some diced cooking apples (1-2 to each cabbage), add finely shredded cabbage, red wine (1 bottle for 100), red wine vinegar (until it all smells kinda vinegary), salt, pepper, bayleaves, maybe some juniper berries, and redcurrant jelly (1jar for 30-40 portions). Cover and cook until the cabbage is soft. Use 1 medium sized cabbage for 20 portions as a side.

Herbed cucumbers: for 50: fry 8 diced cucumbers and 4 large-ish sliced onions a bit, then add fresh herbs (1-2 bunches), nearly ½ a bottle Tabasco, salt, cover and steam for a while longer, stirring occasionally.

Salsa: there's lots of different recipes but the general idea is finely chopped veg with some chopped tomato, lime and/or lemon juice, fresh herbs like coriander and fresh chilli. It's also nice to add some fruit if you can such as finely diced apple, banana or mango.

Pickles, chutneys, jellies, sauces or dips: look in cookbooks (proper ones) and get inspired, or look in the cash and carry or Asian food shops for large pots of nice things.

Roasted veg peelings: If you have an oven, and you're peeling lots of squash, parsnips or other sweet root vegetables, keep the peelings, toss them with oil, salt, and maybe a bit of sugar and roast spread out on an oven tray until crispy and delish. These probably won't make it out of the kitchen.

Snacks

I.e. stuff you'd prep at home or a kitchen you can use, then pack up and take to where you're going, e.g. a demo. Ideally you'll have stuff that's easy to eat with just a napkin, as disposable plates are floppy and wasteful. Also, consider that it'll all be cold, needs to be easily transportable, and shouldn't be in danger of going off and manky in the sun. Funnily enough, people don't seem to want light, posh food at a demo or action - they want filling stuff, and lots of sugar too. It's nice if you can do tea and coffee especially if it's cold - take an insulated urn, or some of those air pot things, or an electric urn if there's leccy somewhere or

a gas powered water boiler. Bring savoury things like sandwiches, nut and other savoury slices, pasties, slices of vegan pizza (still tasty when cold if you used a lot of olive oil), bhajis, samosas, veggie sos rolls or other things in puff pastry cases/rolls, salads in pita breads like tabbouleh, potato, bean, falafels, or salads and tahini in tortilla wraps,... People who are wheat intolerant are buggered though.

Pizza

Ingredients: strong white flour, salt, yeast, sugar, olive oil, onion, garlic, chopped tomatoes, tomato puree, basil/oregano/herbs, pepper, toppings
Optional: semolina, red wine

You need a large oven with good, strong heat for this (or a custom made pizza oven - ooh). A thin base will cook quickly - about 15 minutes - in a hot oven, so you can make them in batches - we've done this over an evening in our social centre as a fundraiser for example. We've also made pizza, cut it in slices, and taken it stacked in a food box with greaseproof paper between layers to feed hungry demonstrators.

To make the dough for 35-40 medium sized slices, use about 1kg/2.2lbs white flour (preferably strong white flour, or a mix of strong white and wholemeal flour; you can also add a bit of semolina for a good texture). Make in batches. Add just about half a tablespoon of salt. If you're using dried active yeast, you can just mix this in, along with a heaped tablespoon of sugar - the amount you need will be noted on the packet. For yeast granules that need activating, boil up some water, dissolve a tablespoon of sugar in it, and mix it with an equal amount of cold water - you'll need nearly two pints altogether, and the water should be lukewarm. Dissolve a couple tablespoons of the yeast in it, cover and leave to stand in a warmish place for about 10 minutes, until a froth has developed on the top. If this doesn't happen, the water might have been too hot so try again.

Then make a dough by adding the yeast mixture and a dash of olive oil bit by bit (or ca. 2 pints lukewarm water if using active yeast), stirring with your hands or with a butterknife (I find this works quite well). It shouldn't be too wet and stick to your hands, or too dry and crumbly, and gradually turn into a dough. Turn it out of the bowl onto a smooth, floured surface and knead for as long as you can be arsed. Push the dough down, fold over, punch down, and repeat, and repeat... Sprinkle a bit of oil into the bowl and return the dough to it, cover with a wet teatowel and put the dough somewhere warm to rise for a couple of hours. The minimum seems to be 1 1/2 hours.

For a tomato sauce for the amount above, finely chop 2 onions and a few cloves of garlic, and fry in a thick bottomed pan. Add some red wine for extra flavour - boil it rapidly for a few minutes which will burn off the alcohol and intensify the taste. Add 2 small tins of chopped tomatoes and a tube of tomato puree. Add a dash of sugar, and lots of herbs - basil and oregano are essential, use either handfuls of dried or finely chopped fresh basil and sprigs of oregano tied with string. Experiment with other herbs over time. Turn

KILL CAPITALISM

BEFORE IT KILLS THE PLANET

down and simmer for as long as possible.

Grease the trays you'll be using (trays with low sides are best, but most trays work fine in a hot oven.) When the dough's risen, knead it and let it rise again for a shorter while. Then tear off a chunk and roll it out with a rolling pin on a smooth floured surface to fit the tray. Pick up the rolled out dough and gently pull it apart with your hands, to stretch it a bit further. If it tears, set it down in the tray and repair it by squidging it back together. Knead the dough up to the edges of the tray, take a tablespoon olive oil and drizzle it over the dough spreading it with the back of the spoon and then spread out a ladleful of tomato sauce thinly.

Now add toppings: sliced red onion, cooked spinach, sliced peppers, sliced mushrooms, sweetcorn, chopped olives, marinated crumbled tofu, any sliced fake meat veggie product, tinned pineapple, fried sliced aubergine or courgette, broccoli florets, fried or roasted sliced leek, thinly sliced, cooked and maybe roasted potato slices (I really like this), tomato slices, fresh herbs, sliced spring onion, a mix of finely chopped olives, capers and fresh chillis.... You can put pretty much anything onto pizza, so experiment! You can also drizzle a 'cheese' sauce over it, see below.

Bake in a very hot oven. They're done when you pick the edges up off the trays without the pizza falling apart. Bear in mind that things take longer to cook if the oven's completely packed, so it may make sense to only do a few at a time but be able to change over more often. If you're serving the pizza cold, make sure the slices are cooled before you pack them away otherwise germs will fester and/or it'll be more likely to go off.

Engevita Sauce: Use equal amounts nutritional yeast flakes (sold in the UK as 'Engevita') mixed with flour (about 500g/1lb each for 60-80 portions); plus a few teaspoons of salt and mix in a saucepan that you know isn't prone to burning. Add up to 4.5 litres/19 cups of water bit by bit, stirring well, bring slowly to the boil stirring constantly then take it off soon after it starts boiling. Whisk in some oil or margarine (again about 500g/1lb) and a few tablespoons of mustard. The sauce will thicken when left to stand so use as soon as possible.

If it goes all clumpy whisk it again or stick a blender in. Drizzle over your pizza before baking, it's also nice over pasta or nachos.

Pasties

They make great filling snack food and are easy to make if you are at all handy with dough and have a good large prep surface to roll it out on. The basic idea is make a pastry – shortcrust or puff pastry – roll it out, cut it into smaller shapes e.g. large rounds or squares that you put some filling into – anything from leftover drained stew to an invented vegetable and pulse combination - then fold over to make a parcel.

Try not to over or underfill - usually, 1 tbsp of filling is enough for a 10x10cm/4"x4" square/round, 3 tbsp for 20x20cm/8"x8". Wet the edges and make sure you press together firmly. It looks nice if you crimp the edges with a fork. Brush the pastry with some soymilk, bake and cool and serve, either hot or cold. You can also cheat and use ready made vegan pastry if you prefer – we often use frozen puff pastry and it actually works out pretty cheap.

Shortcrust Pastry

Use twice the amount of flour to margarine and work it in by rubbing it between your fingers. Work fast or use a food processor to do this. Add salt or other herbs as you wish, then work in some cold water, just a little bit (like a tablespoon) at a time, until the dough holds together. Either use immediately, or wrap in clingfilm and refrigerate before using for 30 minutes up to 24 hours (before rolling it out, leave it at room temperature for 10 minutes). Dust your work surface with a sprinkling of flour then roll out the pastry to the shapes you need. Bake in a medium hot oven for 15-20 minutes.

You can make the pastry richer by adding a bit of soya flour or a dash of lemon juice, or some ground nuts.

Spinach and Tofu Pasty Filling

Ingredients: spinach, onion, garlic, peppers, tofu, oil, oregano, cooked rice, tomato puree, paprika, salt and pepper

To make 24: Cook 5 large bunches of fresh spinach or 4kg/9lbs frozen spinach. Squeeze out the water, then mix with 3 finely diced onions, 3 cloves of minced garlic, 2 finely diced peppers, 1kg/2lbs crumbled firm tofu, a big dash of vegetable oil, oregano, paprika, 2 tubes/1lb tomato puree, salt and pepper and 300g/2 cups cooked rice.

Cakes

There's a lot of recipes for vegan cakes, just look in any vegan cookbook... but the following are the ones that have never failed me, and I think are the most economical.

If you're making one cake, you might as well be making 10 - as long as you have everything you need ready, a decent oven, and enough baking trays. I use loaf tins, or for larger amounts, deep baking trays. Remember to grease them before use, to preheat the oven, and to lick the bowl clean... Cool cakes when you take them out the oven on cooling trays (those bits from grill pans will do), first cool in the tin, then when you can hold the tin without it feeling hot, take a knife and go round the edges, then turn over as quick as possible and pull off. Turn the cake right side up and cool again for quite a while, before you put on icing/cut up and put away. To stack cakes in a tray, use greaseproof layers between the layers but only if the icing's properly set. I've found shoe boxes , stacking vegetable crate style boxes (e.g. the blue mushroom trays) and also flat wide tupperware useful for cake transport.

Vegan Sponge Cake

Ingredients: self raising flour, caster sugar, oil, soymilk, bicarbonate of soda

To fill 2 loaf tins, or 1 medium sized deep baking tray

Step 1: Sift 400g self raising flour (for chocolate cake: 50g cocoa + 350g flour), 200g caster sugar. Mix together.

Step 2: Mix in 200ml sunflower or veg oil

Step 3: Mix separately, then mix in: 300ml soymilk, or 200ml soymilk and 100ml water, 1 teaspoon each bicarbonate of soda and lemon juice or vinegar

Bake at 180-200 degrees (gas mark 5/6) ca. 30 minutes or until a knife stuck in comes out clean.

There's a billion variations. If adding powdery stuff, weigh it off against the flour e.g. 30g ground nuts +370g flour, if it's liquids, weigh it off against the soymilk, e.g 10ml lemon juice + 290ml soymilk), if it's chunky, just mix in.

Variations:

add grated lemon grind in step 1, and more lemon juice in step 3

add chopped dates in step 1 and mashed banana in step 3

add choc chips in choc cake

add ginger in step 1

add grated carrot and maybe some chopped walnuts in step 1 and maybe some desiccated coconut or sultanas in step 3

add rum flavouring to a choc cake in step 3

add tinned pitted cherries after step 1, plus cherry brandy in step 3

add chopped dates and walnuts and/or bananas in step 1

add any combination of dried fruit in step 1

add grated orange rind in step 1 and orange juice in step 3

add nuts, spices....

apple cake: add ½ teaspoon mixed spice in step 1, slice apples finely and arrange on top of poured out dough - it's nice to press the slices in close together, and sprinkle on more mixed spice

marble cake: ½ white dough, ½ choc dough, pour into tin on top of each other and give one gentle stir with a fork

Choc icing: Melt plain chocolate in a bowl set in a pan of simmering water (don't let water come up to the sides of the bowl), use immediately, or stir in soy cream bit by bit until it's fudgey.

Choc mock cream: (enough for recipe above) Heat 3/4 cup caster sugar and 1/3 cup water in a pan, and simmer at least 5 minutes, then cool. Melt 80g/nearly 3oz dark chocolate in a bowl over simmering water. Beat 125g/half a cup marge with electric beater until light, pour cooled sugar water in slowly, beating the whole time, then add melted choc, still beating. Cherry brandy or other alcohol is nice in this.

'Butter' icing: cream margarine (or marge plus a bit of trex or other shortening) with icing sugar with a fork, electric beater or in a food processor and a small dash of soymilk if its not creamy. Add up to a tablespoon of flavouring if you wish, like desiccated coconut, lemon juice, almond essence, coffee, vanilla.

Caramel icing: Boil up 140g/2/3 cup raw cane sugar and 55g/1/4cup marge and 4 tablespoons soymilk or coconut milk until it froths up, simmer for another 3-4 minutes, take off the heat and carry on beating until it gets thicker, add a drop of vanilla essence if you like.

Oat Treats

Ingredients: raw cane sugar, soymilk, cocoa, nuts, rolled oats, dessicated coconut/icing sugar or cocoa powder

Mix 115g/half a cup raw cane sugar, 60ml/1/4 cup soymilk, and 1 heaped tbsp cocoa powder in a pan. Bring to boil while stirring slowly, then simmer for 3 minutes. Chop 30g/1oz nuts, plus some raisins if you like.

Take the pan off the heat and stir in chopped nuts, raisins if using, and 170g rolled oats. Form into walnut sized balls, and roll in dessiccated coconut, icing sugar, cocoa powder or whatever. Refrigerate before serving.

Raw brownies

For a proper sugarfree and raw treat, chuck the following in a food processor: 1 cup walnuts, 1 cup cashew nuts, 1/2 cup cocoa, 24 dates, 1/4 cup raw cacao nibs and a pinch of salt. Squide into a greased tin and chill.

Fridge Cake

Ingredients: margarine, cocoa, golden syrup, digestive biscuits/'graham crackers' Optional: chopped nuts, raisins/dried fruit

Melt 1/2 a pack marge, 1 large cup cocoa powder, ca. 100ml/1/2 cup golden syrup. Off the heat, mix in bit by bit 1 1/2 packets crushed digestive biscuits (put them in a plastic bag, hold shut, and pound with a rolling pin). You could also add a handful of chopped nuts, or chopped up dried fruit if you were so inclined.

Line a tin with greaseproof paper or grease it well, and squidge the mixture into the tin. Refrigerate then serve.

Banana Ice Cream

Ingredients: bananas, soymilk, veg oil, lemon juice, vanilla essence

This is the one ice cream we've made in bulk, ever. It's a good one to do if you find yourself with a ton of bananas. You need an empty freezer, and when you take it out you should use it pretty quickly.

For 40: Chop up to 5kg/11lbs bananas and freeze in plastic boxes for 4 hours. Blend in batches with altogether 1.25l/5 cups soymilk, 750ml/3 cups oil, about half a pint lemon juice, and a small bottle of vanilla essence (mix all the liquids, then add bit by bit to the bananas until you have a good consistency). Serve it with hot chocolate sauce.

Hot Chocolate Sauce

Ingredients: margarine, cornflour, cocoa, soymilk

for 40-50: melt 300g/1 1/3 cup marge over medium heat, add a cup of cornflour bit by bit, and cook for a couple minutes stirring well. Add about 300g/2 2/3 cups cocoa powder and the same amount of sugar, continue heating and stirring. Slowly whisk in in 4l/1 gallon soymilk or a mix of soymilk and water a little at a time, and continue until thickened.

FEEDING THE MASSES AT THE G8

So, the G8 (group of 8 leading industrial countries) met in July 2005 in Scotland. The Dissent! mobilisation against it began two years earlier, and it soon became clear that the best way we could contribute was to start thinking about making sure people would get fed. Being two catering groups based within the movement, Veggies and the Anarchist Teapot formed a catering working group and slowly started compiling information, and reaching out to find other mobile kitchens to help cook for the expected 10 000 or whatever random number was being bandied about.

There were ideas of having various convergence centres over the South of Scotland - in Glasgow and Edinburgh, then also a large rural site that would be the main focus for the blockades planned at the start of the summit. We decided we would also mainly focus on the rural site, because people would be much more dependent on kitchens there than in the middle of a city. Another idea that emerged for the rural convergence site was that it would be divided into `barrios' i.e. neighbourhoods, that would be based around affinity, social centres or geography and would be having their own meetings, as well as their own kitchens. Kitchens and groups both from the UK and abroad started committing themselves to come.

Thankfully, a London based kitchen, Kaos Café, took on the catering at Glasgow, and the Brighton based Café Clandestino who had previously mostly catered at festies but were up for being involved in this mobilisation came forward and took on Edinburgh. This turned out to be difficult and unpredictable to plan for, due to the hassle of finding an autonomous convergence space in Edinburgh in which people could sleep and be fed in. The Teapot decided we would split our kitchen and come help in Edinburgh for a day too, at the council's official campsite in which Dissent! had a space in the end.

The main decisions made amongst kitchens in advance via an email group were: all cooked food would be vegan (though non vegan donations received would be put out for people to take), we would charge for food, 50p for breakfast, £1 for a simple meal and £1.50 for a fuller meal, while not turning away anyone who couldn't afford this, and we would all be putting up money where we could and pooling all takings, and problems with losses or what to do with any potential surplus would be discussed on site before everyone left and shared out as fairly as possible (without anyone making private profit - this was pretty much assumed anyway).

Someone told of how a number of kitchens cooked at the mobilisation in Evian, and that there was a big marquee that acted as a central food storage to which all deliveries came and all donations were brought. We thought that sounded like a good idea for the rural site - if every kitchen were ordering food or sorting supplies for themselves there could be a lot of waste, and combining the efforts sounded much more sensible. The Teapot took on sorting this central food store and ordering in supplies, which turned out to be a bit of a scary task. It involved looking at spending tens of thousands of pounds, guessing numbers coming to site as anything between 500 and 6000, and trying to find suppliers that were willing to cope with potential police hassle, potential orders changed at the last minute, and getting us 1000kg of potatoes...

The money thing was especially frightening. On a scale like this, you can't rely on donations or what you can skip, and you also need money for travel (we definitely wanted to help the kitchens coming from abroad with this), gas, equipment... So after a lot of juggling figures we came up with needing about £12000 upfront for all the initial orders and supplies - even after breaking down orders to as many deliveries we could, and getting a few things like tea and coffee on credit - but we actually managed to raise this by borrowing money from lots of different kitchens and some other campaign groups. We didn't have to tap into other parts of the Dissent! mobilisation at all, and managed to pay everyone back at the end - hurra!

I was really happy with the suppliers we ended up with. A local farmer got us staple veg like potatoes (which he told me was all they ever eat in Scotland), onions, and terrifyingly gigantic carrots, and an organic distributor got us things like salad vegetables and cabbages. Both of them were friendly, amused by trying to get around the police, gave us good discounts and some free extras, and were genuinely interested in what was going on. We ordered wholefoods like dried beans, margarine etc from Green City in Glasgow, who brought 3 deliveries altogether and were really supportive. When you're in a position of having to spend such large amounts of cash, it's much nicer to give the large amounts of cash to people who aren't complete wankers.

One thing that made the ordering difficult was the fact that the site was opening on Friday the 1st July, and that meant any orders for the Monday, to cover feeding people Monday to Wednesday, had to be placed before the Friday. So, we placed the orders without having any idea how many people would be turning up, or what exactly other kitchens would be cooking with, though we'd asked for order lists a number of times beforehand. (Also, not knowing that we would be getting tons and tons of muesli donated - we literally had a muesli mountain about 10 times the size of me in the end).

Finding bread was an ordeal. We weren't fussed about getting organic bread, but we found that, apparently, just normal, properly baked bread isn't very popular in Scotland, you can only get Sunblest and Mothers Pride squidgy white sliced bread... About a day before we left, we had finally found a couple of bakeries that seemed to be able to cover our needs - who actually baked bread, with flour, and no chemicals, and could cope with hundreds of loaves a day. We did slightly overorder and the first few days, we had a giant bread mountain and people got bread with everything. We even made a bread spreads - to put on bread!

As it happened, the rural site wasn't that rural. In fact, it was next to a Morrisons superstore. It wasn't ideal in a lot of ways but there we were. There were a large number of kitchens, mostly able to cater for 100-300+ people in a neighbourhood: the Belgian Kokkerelen collective; an Irish kitchen combining Bitchen Kitchen and Certain  Death Vegan Café; the Scottish Healands kitchen who were already on site when we arrived who we hadn't heard from beforehand; kitchens from the social centres in Bradford (1in12) and Leeds (Common Place, with some Sheffield people too); Veggies from Nottingham; Why don't you from Newcastle; a kitchen from Lancaster with lots of Danish people for some reason; a Bristol kitchen; a kitchen from Oxford; a kitchen in the Queer Barrio; and Purple Penguin from up North who came and baked all day, making lovely vegan cakes and pastries. The Anarchist Teapot teamed up with Rampenplan to form a huge kitchen (Rampenpot, or the Anarchist Plan) to cater for the neighbourhood-less masses, any overspill from neighbourhoods, as well as the separate People and Planet area. This wasn't something we had intended - P+P were insistent on having their own area, and as far as we were concerned we thought they were then also sorting out their own catering. Quite late in the day we heard they didn't have a kitchen - thankfully, it worked out okay because there were less people than there could've been, meaning we could feed an extra 400 without any problems, on top of the 1000 plus we were feeding already.

Our kitchen really was huge. We had a row of 9 giant pans, one of which held 350 litres and when I tried to wash it up I would disappear inside it. We also had the central food store at the back of our marquee. Once on site, we decided to have a kitchen delegates meeting every morning after breakfast, to figure out how it's going, who's cooking lunch and whether every kitchen needed to cook everyday, etc. The other kitchens also would come and pick up ingredients and gas from the store; we also all lent various bits and pieces to each other throughout. It took a few days for all of us to find our feet - some of the kitchens that came hadn't had much experience with mass catering in a field, everyone needed to be set up with what they needed, lots of gas splitters were installed and ditches dug and water needed to be connected up, etc, etc... Everyone seemed to get the hang of it pretty quickly though, and soon we had fantastic food all over the site available at different times (with the Healands kitchen often going all night!). I had been worried we would be too dominant with our huge kitchen and food store, and we would be the 'experts' on site, and in some cases I suppose we were, but generally, each kitchen developed its own individual way of doing things and it felt varied and decentralised.

As a registered food business with insurance and everything, Veggies had taken on dealing with the local authorities. As a legal site in constant negotiation with the local council, this was an aspect we couldn't ignore. The food hygiene inspection happened fairly early on, and went okay (phew!), with us sat there in a very clean marquee in our aprons waiting for them...

The finances were daunting at first - £15000 spent on food and rising, only £7000 taken over the weekend to pay for it... - but then there was a huge influx of people around the Tuesday, the 5th, the day before the mass blockades, and we all found ourselves cooking and cooking, and getting a lot of the money back... In fact, the Rampenpot made soup three times during the night, as well as gallons of coffee. We still had a lot of bread, so all the kitchens put it out with spreads, as well as nuts, seeds, raisins, bits of fruit or whatever else was there, and little bags for people to make themselves packed lunches to take away with them, seeing as lots of people were off to spend the night in the woods to do actions in the morning. All of this went incredibly fast. People were putting vegan mayo and nowt else on their sandwiches when the other spreads ran out...

As it happened, thousands of people went out, did a whole range of generally successful blockades early in the morning, came back to the site where the kitchens were waiting for them with hot food, and loads of people went straight back out again and on to Gleneagles... basically, cool actions happened, we fed them, and it was good.

After the Wednesday, the police decided they needed to control our movement much more and surrounded the site. This led to a feeling of a state of siege,

people started drifting off, and it also led to some comedy attempts to get deliveries of food supplies passed through police lines.

Another thing that started happening around then was that people got ill... Not surprising considering the numbers of people on site and also not surprising that kitchens got blamed for this. The actual reason was the general hygiene, almost certainly overloaded portaloos and a lack of handwashing facilities (a lovely process otherwise known as faecal-oral transmission!) The kitchens were probably the one place people did wash their hands before handling food. Containing the Faecal Oral Transmission (or Dissent!ry) became pretty important so we set up extra handwashes outside each kitchen, and since the kitchens were a place it still could spread further we also changed the washing up system so that it was one or two people doing everyone's washing up, and we pre-sliced bread we served instead of letting everyone handle the loaves to cut it themselves. The lesson here was definitely that kitchens should feel responsible for general hygiene of a site and not just the hygiene in the kitchen, because if it goes wrong, you'll get the blame! The council supplied a whole bunch of alcohol based water free antibacterial handwash. The only thing is though that that stuff doesn't work when exposed to the hot sun.

Anyway, we all survived...

Towards the Friday, there definitely was a feeling of activists leaving and idiots with soundsystems replacing them. That wasn't what we'd come to cook for, and in the kitchen meeting most kitchens seemed to be preparing to leave. After a lot of calculations, paying people back and taking tons of change to the bank in a wheelbarrow, we found out we'd made a surplus of about £5000! It was decided that this should go to other parts of the Dissent! mobilisation and the bulk of it to prisoner support, as well as not letting any kitchen be out of pocket. Mugs, plates and bowls that had strayed were taken back to the kitchens they came from, leftovers divvied up... Then it was time to go home...

The people trying to leave the country with the Dutch kitchen equipment got interrogated under the Terrorism Act for ages on the border - with cops asking questions about how food was organised... They went through everything, including individually searching through 1500 stacked cups! They eventually were left to get on the ferry.

From what we heard, the food was appreciated, and the kitchens were a part of all the infrastructure created for the mobilisation that worked well. And one thing that came out of it is that we now have a lot more action kitchens in the UK who have the ability and the experience to cook for actions, gatherings, and camps.

UK resources

Wholefood suppliers we have ordered from are: (most of these do both organic and non-organic bulk foods but generally better quality than cash and carry supplies):

Suma, Halifax (01422 313861), www.suma.co.uk (deliver almost all over the England and Wales)

Lembas, Sheffield (0845 458 1585), www.lembas.co.uk (deliver 80+ mile radius of Sheffield)

Infinity Foods, Brighton (01273 424060), www.infinityfoods.co.uk (deliver in the South East but also further afield)

Essential, Bristol (0117 958 3550), www.essential-trading.co.uk (deliver all over the South)

Green City, Glasgow (0141 5547633), www.greencity.co.uk (deliver in Scotland)

Other suppliers:

To source your nearest **gas** supplier go to www.calor.co.uk

Search for local suppliers at www.bigbarn.co.uk and organic suppliers at www.soilassociation.org

Veggies have compiled further mass catering advice here: http://www.veggies.org.uk/catering/gatherings/

Glossary

This is a glossary for any Americans who do seem to speak an entirely different language to us in the UK.

Aubergines are eggplants
Bicarbonate of soda is baking soda
Butterbeans are lima beans
Caster sugar is superfine sugar
Chickpeas are garbanzos
Coriander (fresh) is cilantro
Courgettes are zucchinis
Cornflour is cornstarch
To grill is to broil
Haricot beans are navy beans
Icing sugar is powdered sugar
Plain flour is all-purpose flour
A scone is a biscuit. Biscuits are cookies. It's all confusing.
Spring onions are scallions
Swedes (the root vegetable, not the people) are rutabagas
Tomato puree is tomato paste.
Tomatoes are tomaytoes